AMERICA ATTACKED

TERRORISTS DECLARE WAR ON AMERICA

Edited by
Sara Jess,
Gabriel Beck, R. Joseph
Brain-Mind.com
University Press, California

Assistant, Contributing & Copy Editors:
Simon Leung, Tracy Jade,
Rosa Maria Mancini

Jess, Sara
America Attacked: Terrorism, War, America — 1st ed.

ISBN: 0-9700733-7-2

1. Terrorism.   2. War.   3. World Trade Center.   4. Hijackings
5. Osama bin Laden.   6. Mass Murder. 7. Jihad.   8. Holy War

Cover Photo: The New York Post
Back Cover Photos: Associated Press
Photo Credits: Associated Press, Reuters, AFP, Getty Images, the New York Post.
Acknowledgements: Some of the quoted material reproduced in this text was first reported in the New York Post, The New York Daily News, the Los Angeles Times, Associated Press, and Reuters. Vikram Zutschi provided University Press, California, with several eye-witness accounts including those of survivors and rescuers. Dorothy Foglia of Foglia Publications, as always, provided expert technical support.

Portions of the Proceeds from the Sales of this Book Will Be Donated to the Families of the Brave Men & Women Who Lost Their Lives Saving the Lives of Others.

University Press, California
San Jose, California

*Dedicated to the incredibly brave and
courageous men and women of New York City:
firemen, police, rescue workers,
medical personnel, and all those courageous
and fearless souls who risked their lives, and
those who sacrified their lives,
saving the lives of others.*

The Valley of the Shadow of Death

The LORD is my shepherd; I shall not want.

He maketh me to lie down in green pastures: he leadeth me beside the still waters.

He restoreth my soul: he leadeth me in the paths of righteousness for his name's sake.

Yea, though I walk through the valley of the shadow of death, I will fear no evil: for thou art with me; thy rod and thy staff they comfort me.

Thou preparest a table before me in the presence of mine enemies: thou anointest my head with oil; my cup runneth over.

Surely goodness and mercy shall follow me all the days of my life: and I will dwell in the house of the LORD for ever.

CONTENTS

******

"I heard the roar of a Jet and looked out the window... it was coming right at us... There was an explosion....The building shook. Within seconds, you could see debris coming towards the window.

We ran toward the emergency exit.

The stairways were crowded and smoky. Some of the people had been injured. Some were bleeding. Others were burnt,,, all desperately trying to flee, to get out.

The lower 10 to 15 floors were flooded, so we were walking through water as firemen were walking up.

Once we got outside, we saw dozens of people jumping out of the building. From the top floor. 1000 feet up. Some of them were on fire.

There were screams, cries. I ran into the street, and watched in horror as six people either fell or jumped, dropping like dolls from the upper floors.

Everyone was running -cops, firefighters, civilians.

Suddenly the top of the tower just shattered into thousands of pieces. The walls peeled away. The entire structure, once standing over 100 floors tall, folded into itself like a house of cards. Then the smoke came billowing down the streets like a solid wall of darkness coming right at you... it scared the shit out of me.

The cops started yelling, "Get back! Run! Get away!" I ran inside a hotel. Everything went black outside, because of the dust.

People were screaming and diving for cover. Others wandered around like ghosts, weeping and covered in dirt."

— A Survivor

******

THE MIND OF THE TERRORIST

The terrorist is a predator, probing for weakness, spawning fear and horror in order to sap and destroy the will of a people.

The object of terror is to instill terror and force capitulation. Through fear and terror one can demand obedience and blind submission.

Terror is a form of propaganda. It is a political weapon.

Nightmarish fear, the uncertainty of death, becomes an unceasing pounding pounding pounding that begins with the heart and ends with the soul.

Terrorism is a form of violence committed against the soul... Terror shocks the system, wearing one down, forcing one to recoil in horror and to submit.

Through death and terror (and the promise of more deaths to come), the terrorist hopes to conquer all opposition. Terror is a political weapon and its purpose is to force capitulation.

Through fear, brutality and physical terror, the terrorist hopes to gain mastery over the soul and the mind of the people. And when terror is followed by yet more terror, the psychological effect can be calculated with an almost mathematical precision.

Terror at the place of employment, in the factory, in the streets, on the playground, if followed by yet more terror, will almost always achieve its aims, which is withdrawal and submission—unless opposed by equal terror.

If terror is followed by yet more mindless terror, if the people are faced with the uncertainty of death, victory can be achieved as the defeated adversary in most cases, despairs of the success of any further resistance. The terrorist and his cohorts see each death and each act of unspeakable violence as a victory for their cause.

Cruelty is impressive. Cruelty and brutal strength appears

unstoppable. It shocks the system and makes a lasting impression, leading almost always to surrender. In the mind of the terrorist, the opposition, the public, his enemies, need the thrill of terror to make them shudderingly submissive.

Terror is the most effective form of politics.

The terrorist believes that terror is always the most effective form of war and the most effective argument against further resistance. Those who are terrorized are easily swayed and are willing to do your bidding.

The opposition must feel fear and terror. Uncertainty is essential. They must never know if they or their loved ones will be maimed or murdered. They must always feel they are at risk of suffering a horrible death. They must always feel as if the iron hand of terror may strike at any moment, for any reason, or for no reason at all. They or their neighbors may be killed or maimed at any time, at any place—at home, in bed, while making love, while kissing their children good night.

The important thing in spreading terror is an over-whelming and contagious fear of suffering horrific injuries and a nightmarish death.

Through the uncertainty of terror, the people become compliant, fearful and overwhelmed by incomprehensible anxiety, and are thus easily led and swayed.

When terror is followed by more terror, the people become afraid to continue their everyday routines, they become paralyzed and are no longer able to resist the terrorist's agenda.

Through calculated, institutionalized terror, the opposition and the enemy, will surrender because capitulation offers the only possibility of salvation.

Violence begets violence. Through brutality, physical terror and violence we are able to gain mastery over the soul and the mind of our enemies. We win by making them afraid.

******

"I was having a cup of coffee in my office on the 82nd floor of the south Tower, reading my e-mail, when the first jet hit. I heard the explosion. I was startled. I spilt my coffee.

We faced the north Tower. I could see smoke and flames through the window. I thought a bomb had gone off.

It didn't occur to me that we were in any danger. My partner and I got up to take a closer look.

Thick black smoke was billowing out of the side of the north Tower. The windows were busted out. I could see fires raging inside the upper floors.

Men and women were dashing about wildly. They were gathering at the broken windows. Dozens of people, hundreds of people standing at the windows, looking out, staring down at the ground, 1000 feet below, as the fires raged behind them.

More and more of them were crowding at the windows. They were gesturing, waving their arms frantically, suffocating, drowing in the billowing black smoke.

The fires were spreading, leaping from floor to floor. I could see tongues of flame licking at the windows.

Some of the men, even tried to climb out.

That's when they began jumping.

I couldn't believe it. I thought I would vomit.

They were leaping from the windows to escape the flames.

Dozens of them... leaping, falling, a thousand feet down... Some of them burning and in flames."

— *A Survivor*

******

THE KAMIKAZE-TERRORIST

During World War II, hundreds of Japanese pilots used their planes as guided missiles to strike U.S. warships. They were called Kamikaze: the Divine Wind.

In 1281, Genghis Khan was leading the Mongols on an overwhelming attack against Japan and just as it seemed the Japanese were defeated, a great typhoon swept through the land, destroying the entire Mongol Army. It was a Divine Wind: Kamikaze.

In 1944, it had become increasingly clear the Japanese were losing the war with the United States. In October 1944, the Japanese General Staff decided that the only way to stave off certain defeat was by mounting organized suicide attacks.

The Kamikaze subsequently destroyed or sank 56 American and "enemy" ships.

Unlike the divine wind that destroyed Genghis Khan and the Mongol armies, the Kamikaze were unable to halt the march of the Americans and their allies.

The Japanese first employed suicide attacks during the assault on Pearl Harbor. Having run out of bombs and ammunition, or lacking sufficient fuel to make a return flight, a few Japanese pilots willingly crashed their planes into American ships. Yet others, used their bombers to crash into American aircraft, destroying the American target and killing themselves. These suicidal acts were spontaneous and completely voluntary.

In 1944, the General Staff decided to begin organizing massive suicide attacks: "Tokkotai." Their purpose was not only to destroy American battleships, but to attack the Americans psychologically. The purpose was to strike terror directly into the hearts of the Americans and make them lose their will to continue fighting the war.

Minister of the Japanese Navy, Admiral Onishi, also believed it would give his fliers an opportunity "to die beautifully... to make death beautiful."

On October 21, 1944, the first mass Kamikaze suicide attack was made on American ships by a Japanese fighter squadron called the Shinpu Tokubetsu, or in abbreviated form for public consumption, the Tokkotai. "Tokkotai" thereafter became synonymous, in the Japanese mind, with suicide attacks.

Captain Yukio Seki, led the first Kamikaze attack, during the battle off Samos, on the American aircraft carrier Saint Lo. Twelve Japanese fighter planes served as escorts and the others were to become guided missiles aimed at the Saint Lo.

Kamikaze pilots of the Imperial Army ranged from 17 years to 35 years in age, although the majority, were in their late teens or early twenties. Vast numbers of Japanese youth volunteered to become Kamikaze. There were more volunteers than there were planes. The Army selected only those who "earnestly desired" to die, by suicide for their country, and their Emperor, who was a "god."

Those who served the Emperor and became human bombs believed they would enter paradise and be happy forever. In letters home, most Kamikaze pilots declared they were happy and proud to have been allowed to participate in so honorable a mission.

"I received the thankful command to depart tomorrow," wrote a young Kamikaze to his parents. "I am deeply emotional and just hope to sink one American battleship. Already, hundreds of visitors had visited us. Cheerfully singing the last season of farewell."

Enthusiasm however, was not enough. The Kamikaze were given instructions in the spiritual rewards they could expect and attended "Spiritual Moral Lectures," every other day.

In addition to paradise and spiritual morality, many of the Kamikaze were motivated by revenge and a desire to save their country from the invading, all conquering Americans.

In a letter home, second Lieutenant Shigeyuki Suzuki wrote: "People say that our feeling is of resignation, and think of us as a fish about to be cooked. But they do not know at all how we feel. Young blood does flow in us. There are persons we love, we think of, and we have many unforgettable memories. However, with those, we cannot win the war. To let this beautiful Japan keep growing, Japan must be released from the wicked hands of the Americans and British, if we are to build a 'free Asia.' The great day that we can directly be in contact with the battle is our day of happiness and at the same time, the memorial of our death."

On the day of the attacks, the Kamikaze seemed to all who observed them, to be calm, normal, peaceful, to have no fear of death and to be happy that this glorious day had finally come.

The Kamikaze was dying for a cause: To serve God and country.

In the Middle East, the suicide bomber believes he too, is fighting for his country —the establishment of a Palestinian state. But he also believes he is fighting the enemies of god: Israel and America—the Great Satan.

Yet the suicide bomber differs from the Kamikaze. He is not interested in killing soldiers, but civilians. He has no qualms, nor issues about destroying the innocent. Women and children are viable, desirable targets. By bringing the war off the battlefield and into the homes, work and public spaces of the innocent, the suicide bomber tries to spread so much terror that the enemy, who they call Israel, will withdraw from their lands and capitulate, as capitulation offers the possibility of salvation.

Like the Kamikaze, suicide bombers are usually educated young men who have a reverence for god and country. They are often in their late teens and 20s. And like the Kamikaze, who volunteered to die because their cause was nearly hopeless and their country was facing defeat, the suicide bomber is similarly overwhelmed by hopelessness and defeat. He who volunteers to destroy himself and others with a bomb strapped to his back, generally faces a future that offers little hope and only the prospect of humiliation by the Israelis, and failure.

The suicide bomber seeks revenge. The suicide bomber seeks to drive the hated Jews, the invaders, from their country. The suicide bomber believes that through hatred and violence, by murdering innocent people, he is fulfilling a moral and spiritual quest that will lead to martyrdom and paradise.

Most, but not all, suicide bombers are highly religious. Prospects are recruited from mosques and religious institutions and are led to believe that by killing themselves and others, they will go straight to paradise, where they will be seated in honor, next to their almighty God.

According to Islamic tradition, and as taught by "suicide teacher" Mohammed el Hattab, "He who gives his life for Islam will have his sins forgiven and will attain the highest state of paradise." And what is paradise? 70 virgins who will love him and him alone. Eternal sexual bliss is one of the rewards of martyrdom.

Suicide bombers are commonly recruited by and are affiliated with the Palestinian militant group Hamas.

They are recruited from mosques and schools. It is not the brave and courageous who are enticed, but those who appear lonely, troubled, shy and withdrawn—those who might leap at the chance to be accepted, to be part of a group, to be given a mission in life, to feel important, and to belong.

Islamic Jihad also runs a summer school for young boys. The curriculum? Little boys are taught the benefits of becoming suicide bombers. The boys learn that it is good to kill and that it is good to die for your country.

Mohammed, a 14-year-old Palestinian boy, proudly displays a picture he has drawn of himself with explosives strapped to his adolescent body. Mohammed says he is eager and ready to blow himself to pieces if it means killing Jews. "I want to liberate Palestine and be part of the revolution. I want to be a martyr!"

Hasan, a 12-year-old boy also wishes to be a martyr:

"I will make my body a bomb that will blast the flesh off the Zionists. I will blow their bodies into little pieces."

"We are teaching the children that suicide bombing is the only thing that can frighten the Israeli people. We are teaching them that we have the right to kill Jews," said Islamic Jihad member Mohammed el Hattab, one of the teachers.

Similar to most little boys throughout the world, Palestinian youths are naturally excited by heroics and bravado. They want to be brave. Most want to be fighters, and for many little boys, fighting and dying are every day games.

And like their American counterparts, who flock to scary movies and are glued to their violent video games, little Palestinian boys are fascinated by violence. With no real understanding of death and dying, to kill oneself, to kill others, seems to many to be just a game.

"Children come up to me and say, "Conduct another bombing and free our country," says Sheik Hasan Yosef, one of the leaders of Hamas.

But it is not a game. Terror and violence are a form of propaganda and a political weapon. Children are educated to believe that, "yes—you too can be a be a martyr."

In the elementary schools and kindergartens founded by Hamas, there are signs on the wall that read: "The children are the martyrs of tomorrow."

A poster on the wall at Islamic University in Gaza City proclaims: "Israel has nuclear bombs. We have human bombs."

In their classes, young boys and young men are taught and repeatedly reminded that Israel is "illegally occupying our land" and that Jews are racists who treat the Palestinians with ruthless barbarism.

Mohammed el Hattab and Sheik Hasan Yosef say there are hundreds of Palestinian "freedom fighters" who aspire for martyrdom by blowing themselves up, killing Jews, and by "dying for their country." Their hope is to free their homeland by driving out the Jews, who, according to the United Nations, are illegally occupying their lands.

The peoples of Israel believe otherwise. They too have god on their side, for it is their god who gave them this land.

"Great and goodly cities, which thou didst not build and houses full of all good things which thou didst not fill, and cisterns hewn, which thou didst not hew, and vineyards and olive-trees, which thou didst not plant, and thou shalt eat and be satisfied."
— Deuteronomy 6:10-11.

"The Lord thy God shall bring thee into the land, and shall cast out many nations before thee, the Hittite, and the Gergashite, and the Amorite, and the Canaanite, and the Perizzite, and the Hivite, and the Jebusite... and the Lord thy god shall deliver them up before thee, and thou shalt smite them, then thou shall utterly destroy them."
—Deuteronomy 7:1-2.

"Of the cities of these peoples, that the Lord thy God giveth thee for an inheritance, thou shalt save alive nothing that breathest."
—Deuteronomy, 20:16.

"...when you approach a town, you shall lay seizure to it, and when the Lord your god delivers it into your hand, you shall put all its males to the sword. You may, however, take as your booty the women, the children, the livestock, and everything in the town—all its spoils—and enjoy the spoil of your enemy, which the Lord your god gives you.... In the towns of the people which the Lord your god is giving you as a heritage, you shall not let a soul remain alive."
—Exodus 20:15-18   —Deuterotomy 20:12-16

God gave them this land, and the Israelis wholeheartedly believe the Palestinians have no right to it.

Yet the Palestinians believe otherwise, and, like the Kamikaze are willing to die for their cause.

Yet, unlike the Kamikaze, Palestinian suicide bombers wish to murder and maim innocent women and children. They kill indiscriminately. Terror is their weapon.

Israeli officials believe Hamas has several dozen young men, ages 18 to 23, who have been recruited, trained and who eagerly await orders to carry out these suicide attacks.

Terrorists seek not just to kill, but to obtain publicity. Every well-publicized atrocity is a victory for their cause.

Groups, like the Iranian-backed Lebanese Shia'a militant group Hezbollah, are acutely media-conscious. Their targets and the timing of their terrorist attacks are meticulously planned to achieve the maximum public impact. They want to shock. They want to cause outrage. The more audacious and gruesome, the better.

Hezbollah has been in the media-terrorist business for decades.

Hezbollah, an Iranian-backed guerrilla force based in southern Lebanon, are suspected of involvement in the 1983 bombings against the U.S. Marine barracks in Lebanon and the U.S. Embassy. Over 200 U.S. Marines were killed, many while sleeping in their bunks. The United States withdrew from Lebanon soon thereafter.

From the perspective of Hezbollah, terrorist attacks work and they had won.

Hezbollah has also sought to hijack commercial jetliners and crash them into cities. In 1986, Hezbollah hijacked a TWA airliner with the intention of slamming it into buildings in Tel Aviv.

September 11, 2001, is a date that may live in infamy, for generations to come. Yet the use of Kamikaze terrorists to hijack commercial planes, or the use of kamikaze warriors to slam airplanes into American targets, is not a new or recent stratagem.

A WORLD OF TERRORISM

September 11, 8:45 a.m., American Airlines Flight 11, a Boeing 767 en-route from Boston's Logan Airport to Los Angeles International with 92 people onboard, is hijacked by five men, and slams into the north tower of the World Trade Center.

September 11, 9:03 a.m., United Airlines Flight 175, a Boeing 767 en-route from Boston to Los Angeles with 65 people onboard, is hijacked by five men, and pierces the south tower of the World Trade Center.

September 11, 9:43 a.m., American Airlines Flight 77, a Boeing 757 en-route from Dulles Airport outside Washington to Los Angeles, with 58 passengers and six crew members, is hijacked by five men, and crashes into the Pentagon.

******

The leaders of Hamas, Islamic Jihad, and Hezbollah, as well as several other potential suspect organizations, have repeatedly denied involvement with the September 11 terrorist attacks on America. They say they had nothing to do with the hijackings or the terrorists who smashed into the Pentagon, or the Twin Towers of the World Trade Center.

The spiritual leader of the Islamic Resistance Movement, or Hamas, denied any connection with the attacks, saying, "Our battle is with Israel. Our battles are fought on the Palestinian land."

There is no strong evidence to suggest the members of Hamas played any role in these barbarous assaults on the citizens of the United States.

The same is not true of Hezbollah, which also goes by the name of Islamic Jihad. The U.S. government strongly suspects that Hezbollah was directly involved in the bombings of the U.S. Embassy and U.S. Marine barracks in Beirut in 1983. The purpose of these bombings was to drive U.S. forces from Lebanon. They succeeded.

Despite blustery rhetoric, the Reagan administration cut their losses and pulled their forces from this Muslim country—thus driving home an important lesson to all terrorist organizations, including Hezbollah: terrorism works.

One of the best predictors of the future is the past. And in the past, Hezbollah used terrorist assaults to kill sleeping Americans.

They are not alone.

Numerous other terrorist organizations share a hatred for America, our freedom and our values. Each could have played a major or supportive role in this nightmare of violence.

The list of terrorist organizations throughout the world is enormous. These include Abu Sayyaf, the Armed Islamic Group, Al-Gama'a al-Islamiyya, Harakat ul-Mujahidin, Al-Jihad, Mujahedin-e Khalq, Palestine Liberation Front, Popular Front for the Liberation of Palestine, and al-Qa'eda which is led and financed by Osama bin Laden.

According to the U.S. State Department, what all these groups have in common are their fanatical Islamic beliefs and anti-American anti-Western sentiments.

They could have acted alone or as co-conspirators.

The least likely to have played a major role in the attack on the Twin Towers and the Pentagon is Abu Sayyaf. The loudly voiced goal of Abu Sayyaf is the establishment of an independent Islamic state in the southern Philippines and the overthrow of the pro-Western government which is currently in power.

Likewise, there is little evidence to suggest participation by the Armed Islamic Group that is headquartered in Algeria. The Armed Islamic Group has so far directed their ferocious violence on their fellow citizens, attacking villages and killing and cutting off the heads of women and children. They murder and justify their actions in the name of their god and began their terrorist activities after the pro-Western military establishment of Algiers, voided the electoral victory of the country's largest Islamic opposition party in 1992. Their stated goal is to make Algeria an Islamic state. They hope to accomplish this by maiming and beheading women and children.

Hamas, Islamic Jihad, and Hezbollah, plead innocence. Likewise, the Popular Front for the Liberation of Palestine which is located in Syria, and the Democratic Front for the Liberation of Palestine, which is headquartered in Iraq, categorically deny any involvement.

Can terrorists be taken at their word?

Is there honor among murderers and thieves?

The Popular Front for the Liberation of Palestine has participated in numerous international terrorist attacks against Israel and moderate Arab states. The Palestine Liberation Front is directly responsible for the attack on the Achille Lauro cruise ship in 1985 during which an American passenger was killed and dumped overboard. Both organizations share the goal of an Independent Palestinian state, a goal, which they believe can only be achieved by the destruction of Israel and by proxy, attacks on Israel's only ally, the United States.

The Palestine Liberation Front has a major bone to pick with America. Headquartered in Iraq, the leadership of the Palestine Liberation Front experienced first hand the unbridled wrath and military power of the United States, which devastated Iraq and killed perhaps over 100,000 Iraqi soldiers and tens of thousands of civilians during the Gulf War; casualties which the U.S. refers to as "collateral damage."

The citizens of Iraq continue to suffer from the sins of their leader, Saddam Hussein. Sanctions maintained and enforced by the U.S. have crippled the Iraqi economy, and poverty and the mal-nourishment and death of children have become a part of every day life.

Revenge is often bitterly sweet, and the leaders of the Palestine Liberation Front and the leader of Iraq, Saddam Hussein, thirst for revenge.

Saddam Hussein, has offered a million dollar reward to any-one who shoots or brings down a U.S. plane—a reward that may have been promised to the families of any terrorist who success-fully hijacks a U.S. plane and extracts revenge on America for the devastation caused by the Gulf War.

The promise of significant financial rewards to the families of suicide bombers is believed to be a powerful incentive to those who carry out suicide attacks in Israel. And with Saddam Hussein promising to financially reward the families of suicide bombers it has become a financially lucrative task.

Money! The root of all evil.

Those who led and participated in the assault on the Penta-gon and the World Trade Center, were rolling in dough. They flashed wads of cash wherever they would go. Yet, even despite their lavish spending, they could not spend the money fast enough. Over half a million dollars remained in their bank ac-counts after the attack.

Where did the money come from? Osama bin Laden? Saddam Hussein?

According to former CIA Director James Woolsey, Saddam Hussein has been linked to a number of terrorist operations against the United States, including the 1993 bombing of the World Trade Center.

And again, one of the best predictors of the future, is the past.

A senior U.S. official has reported that there is no evidence which directly links Iraq to the September 11th hijackings. How-ever, that is not exactly true. One of the hijackers, Mohamed Atta, met with Iraqi intelligence officers earlier this year.

Yet, even if Saddam was a major player, this does not mean he played alone.

What other organizations or countries wish to cause immea-surable harm and suffering to the peoples of the United States?

Harakat ul-Mujahidin, Al-Jihad, and al-Qa'eda.

Harakat ul-Mujahidin is fanatically anti-West and anti-American. Although its stated goal is ending India's control of the disputed region of Kashmir and the establishment of a pure Islamic state, it is fanatically anti-American. This organization is also linked to al-Qa'eda, the terrorist army led and financed by Osama bin Laden.

One of the leaders of Harakat ul-Mujahidin, Fazlur Rehman Khalil, cosigned one of Osama bin Laden's fatwas (religious decrees) against the United States, calling for a holy war against America.

Harakat ul-Mujahidin also has some expertise in hijackings. This group is believed responsible for the hijacking of an Indian aircraft in December 2000.

Al-Jihad is a shadowy group, with operatives and agents in Afghanistan, Lebanon, Pakistan, Sudan, Yemen, and the United Kingdom. Its stated goals include the overthrow of the current Egyptian government and the establishment of an Islamic state.

Al-Jihad is responsible for the assassination of Egyptian President Anwar Sadat in 1981. Sadat was killed, in part, because he signed a peace treaty with Israel and because of his pro-western views. The message was violently clear: Cozy up to America and Israel, and you shall die.

Like Harakat ul-Mujahidin, Al-Jihad maintains a close association with bin Laden.

Islamic Jihad, one of the most feared terrorist groups in the world, also maintains an intimate relationship with bin Laden and his al-Qa'eda organization. In January of this year Ayman al-Zawahiri, the head of Egyptian Islamic Jihad, was among the guests at the wedding of bin Laden's son, Muhammad, at a secret ceremony in Afghanistan.

One of the best predictors of the future is the past and those who do not learn from the past, are often condemned to repeat it.

Omar Abdel-Rahman, the leader of yet another terrorist group, Al-Gama'a al-Islamiyya, is currently in jail for the 1993 bombing of New York's World Trade Center. Those who bombed the World Trade Center in 1993 were associated with bin Laden, who, as intelligence sources report, provided considerable financial support, as did militants in Iran.

All roads lead to Osama bin Laden.

Bin Laden and his organization, al-Qa'eda, may well be the key to unraveling the mystery as to who masterminded, orchestrated, planned and executed the attack on America.

Like other Islamic-terrorist groups, the stated goal of al-Qa'eda and bin Laden is to expel non-Muslims from Muslim countries and to overthrow U.S.-allied regimes in the Arab world.

In February 1998, bin Laden said it was the duty of all Muslims to kill U.S. citizens and their allies.

ALL ROADS LEAD TO
OSAMA BIN LADEN

Nineteen men took part in the hijacking of the four doomed commercial jetliners on September 11, 2001. Although there is some dispute about their true identities, more than half of the men have distinctive tribal names from southwest Saudi Arabia. Two others bear Yemeni names.

Yemen is joined at the waist with Saudi Arabia.

Osama bin Laden, who founded and funds the hydra-headed terrorist organization al-Qa'eda, is a Saudi national whose family comes from Yemen. His tribe and family roots are intimately tangled with the tribes that spawned at least half the hijackers.

Then there is the Afghanistan connection.

Osama bin Laden and al-Qa'eda, are headquartered in the remote mountains of Afghanistan. Bin Laden, the multi-millionaire son of a Saudi construction magnate, first aligned himself with the Afghanistan mujahedeen and the Taliban, during the Soviet invasion of Afghanistan. He provided arms, funds, and training and is credited by the leaders of Afghanistan with having provided major assistance in driving the godless communists out of the country.

One of the hijackers, Ziad Jarrah, who presumably piloted United Airlines Flight 93, spent 5 weeks in Afghanistan before coming to the United States.

Waleed M. Alshehri and Wail Alshehri, are brothers who are believed to be from Saudi Arabia . They are members of a clan that fought in Afghanistan during the 1980s.

Bin Laden and his organization al-Qa'eda have been linked to a number of terrorist attacks against the United States.

According to Bin Laden, his god-given mission is to commit mass murder in the name of freedom, justice and Allah.

"Every American man is my enemy."

His overarching goal is to drive America from the Holy Lands and to bring to an end America's military and economic world dominance.

To fulfill this quest, he has sought to kill not only military personnel but also innocent civilians. In his eyes, every American man, woman and child are a potential target.

Tangled are the roots.

Astonishingly, Osama bin Laden, was considered by the U.S. government and the Reagan administration to be an ally and one of our dearest friends.

Osama bin Laden was a partner in the fight against communism and the cold war battles being waged against the Soviet Union.

"The enemy of my enemy is my friend."

In the early 1970s, Afghanistan was being actively considered for international aid and assistance. "A model for development," recalled Amir Usman, a Pakistani ambassador to Afghanistan.

A lot of countries wanted a piece of the action.

Added Amir, "The Americans built the Kabul-Torkham road leading east to Pakistan and the Russians built the road to the Amu Darya leading north to the then-Soviet Union. It was a happy coexistence."

When it came to the Soviety Union, however, happy coexistence was not the aim of American foreign policy.

The ulterior goals of the United States were not so much to aid in the development of Afghanistan but to drive out or at least greatly diminish Soviet influence.

However in 1973, the Soviets gained the upper hand when a series of coups brought down Afghani King Mohammed Zahir Shah. A Marxist dictatorship later came to power in 1978.

The people of Afghanistan are conservative Muslims and the atheist Marxist control of their nation was viewed as an insult to god. The Afghan people resisted the godless invaders and sought to overthrow the Marxist and bring King Mohammed Zahir Shah back to power.

There ensued a decade-long war of national resistance.

The United States began pouring money and arms into Afghanistan, $2 billion during the 1980s; funds and equipment that not only helped force the Soviet forces to withdraw in 1989, but which left the country in shambles. American aid and arms contributed to the destruction of Afghanistan and its capital, Kabul.

Once the Soviets left town and returned home, America lost interest. The Afghan people were left impoverished and adrift.

The perception among the Afghan leadership and other Arab leaders was that America never had any true interest in helping the Afghan people. Nor did the U.S. really want the Soviets to pull out.

The Americans, or so it was believed, wanted the war in Afghanistan to continue indefinitely, so as to keep Soviet forces bogged down and hemorrhaging men and money.

If the country was destroyed, and if tens of thousands of Afghani were killed and maimed, then that was the price that had to be paid in order to fight communism and the red menace. Afghanistan was a battleground where the Soviets could be attacked without risking American lives.

The death of Afghani civilians, and the destruction of Afghanistan was not a concern of American foreign policy makers. The death of Afghani women and children was written off by America as "collateral damage."

Once the Soviet forces withdrew, American interest and American funds nearly vanished. There was very little, if any interest, in helping the impoverished country recover and rebuild.

At the conclusion of the "Cold War," America completely lost interest in Afghanistan. The people were abandoned to their fate—a fate that had been carved out in the bedrock of American foreign policy. The Afghans had been sacrificed on the altar of

America's strategic self-interests.

The country was physically and emotionally destroyed and the people were left with poverty and despair—fertile ground for a fundamentalist Islamic resurgence and those offering a better life. The Taliban quickly stepped into the void. They offered hope and they eventually took power in Kabul.

Islamic fundamentalism is an anathema to the West. When the fundamentalists came to power, the Clinton administration sought to undermine and openly attacked the Taliban government. Afghanistan was to be treated as a potential enemy. The Clinton administration began to actively lobby against international financial aid for Afghanistan.

Afghani despair was eventually transformed into hatred, hatred for the West and hatred for America.

In the eyes of the Afghani people and other Arab communities, America had once again declared war against Muslims and the entire Islamic religion.

Many Arabs believed that Clinton's policy was yet another cynical ploy to inflict harm on their people. The Muslims believed America wanted to keep them oppressed, while allowing the Jewish State of Israel to prosper and grow.

In the eyes of the Arab community, American sentiments were clear: support for Israel, support for Israeli aggression, terrorism and atrocities, and hatred for Arabs and their Islamic religion.

Many Arabs also believed that America's anti-Arab policies were being dictated by the incredible number of Jews working in the Clinton administration. Although President Clinton loved to preach the virtues of diversity and although Jews make up less than 3% of the U.S. population, over 50% of his senior advisors and administrative officials were Jewish:

Secretary of State Madeleine Albright, Secretary of the Treasury Robert Rubin, Secretary of Defense William Cohen, CIA Chief George Tenet, Head of National Security Council Samuel Berger, Secretary of Agriculture Dan Glickman, Chief of NASA Daniel Goldin, Chairman of the Federal Reserve Board Alan

Greenspan, Health Care Chief Sandy Kristoff, Head of Voice of America Evelyn Lieberman, Under Secretary of State for Europe Stuart Elsenstat, U.S. Trade Representative Charlene Barshefsky, Chief Aide to the First Lady Susan Thomases, National Economic Council Gene Sperling, National Health Care Policy Ira Magaziner, Deputy Secretary of State, Peter Tarnoff, Ass. Sec. of State for Congressional Affairs Wendy Sherman, Board of Economic Council Alice Rivlin, Board of Economic Council Janet Yellen, Presidential Advisor Rahm Emanuel, Council to the President Doug Sosnik, Deputy National Security Council Jim Steinberg, NSC Senior Director for Speechwriting Anthony Blinken, Drug Policy Coordinator Robert Weiner, Special Liaison to the Jewish Community Jay Footlik, Presidential Personal Chief Robert Nash, Presidential Attorney Jane Sherburne, Asian Expert on Security Council Mark Penn, Communications Aide Robert Boorstine, Communications Aide Keith Boykin, Special Assistant to the President Jeff Eller, National Health Care Advisor Tom Epstein, National Security Council Judith Feder, Assistant Secretary of Veterans Affairs Richard Feinberg, Deputy Head of Food and Drug Administration Herschel Gober, White House council Steve Kessler, Assistant Secretary of Education Ron Klein, Director of Press Conferences Margaret Hamburg, Director of State Department Policy Karen Alder, National Security Council Samuel Lewis and Stanley Ross, Director of the Peace Corps Dan Shifter, Deputy Chief of Staff Eli Segal, Deputy Director of Man. and Budget Jack Lew, Under Secretary of State James P. Rubin, Under Secretary of the Treasury David Lipton Special Council to the President Lanny P. Breuer, Special Representative to NATO Richard Holbrooke, Chief of Social Security Kenneth Apfel, Deputy White House Council Joel Klein, Special Advisor to the First Lady Sidney Blumenthal, Chief of Food and Drug Administration David Kessler , Acting Solicitor General Seth Waxman, Presidential Pollster Mark Penn, Special Middle East Representative Dennis Ross, General Counsel for the FBI Howard Shapiro, White House Special Counsel Lanny

Davis, Secretary of Management and Budget Sally Katzen, Heads FBI Equal Opportunity Office Kathleen Koch, Deputy Chief of Staff John Podesta, Vice Chairman of Federal Reserve Board Alan Blinder, Council of Economic Advisors Jane Yellen...and the list goes on and on.

Arabs complained and questioned: Why were there no Arabs holding positions of influence in the Clinton Administration? Why does U.S. policy in the Middle East favor the Jew?

One answer might be: Because Israel does not commit terrorist acts against America.

Another might be: Because Israel is a democracy whereas the Arab states are ruled by dictators, tyrants and kings.

Of course, U.S. policy has often favored dictators, tyrants, and kings—that is, when it is in the best interests of the U.S. to do so.

******

"Politics makes strange bedfellow."

Yet, just as a "bedfellow" may awake in the morning only to recoil at those he or she discovers in their bed, the U.S. government has repeatedly awakened with a giddy hangover, aghast at those who she allowed beneath the covers.

Like Saddam Hussein, Manuel Noreiga, Ho Chi Minh, etc., etc., etc., Osama bin Laden was once a very dear friend.

The CIA had long ago climbed into bed with Osama bin Laden and provided him and many other "terrorists" with funding and aid.

Now like so many other "friends," Osama bin Laden has viciously turned against us.

Osama bin Laden came to the aid of the people of Afghanistan in their war to drive out the Soviet dictatorship. But unlike the U.S., which liked to kiss and run, Osama bin Laden made a committment which he honored.

In the 1980s, Osama bin Laden and other individuals and

groups the U.S. now brands as "terrorists" had been proclaimed by the Reagan administration to be "valiant and courageous Afghan freedom fighters."

It was not just praise, but money and arms the U.S. lavished on those who would soon become our "enemies."

Indeed, during the 1980s, the CIA recruited "freedom fighters" from throughout the Islamic world. The CIA provided them with funds, arms and training in terrorist tactics and then instructed them to go forth and wreak havoc.

Bin Laden was particularly attractive to the CIA, most especially because of the close ties his father had established with the Saudi royal family.

Osama bin Laden became our man in Afghanistan.

With his connections, his wealth, and the support and financial backing of the U.S., Osama bin Laden was welcomed into the arms of the power elite throughout much of the Arab world, which in turn enabled him to extend his own power and reach.

The United States assisted in making bin Laden what he is today. The U.S. provided the resources and the many of the connections that enabled him to create his hydra-headed terrorist organization, al-Qa'eda.

No fool, bin Laden, he has always been mindful of U.S. support for Israel's anti-Arab policies. But, you don't look a gift-horse in the mouth especially when it comes bearing arms, money and advanced weaponry. Bin Laden was happy and content to be the beneficiary of so much American generosity.

Once the cold war ended, and the people of Afghanistan were abandoned by the U.S. to their sorrowful fate, bin Laden continued to use his considerable wealth and influence to fight the enemies of Islam and to benefit his adopted people.

******

Bin Laden did not turn against his former "friend" and benefactor, the United States, until the onset of the Persian Gulf War.

Bin Laden was of two minds regarding the invasion of Kuwait by Iraq's Saddam Hussein. Although he opposed Iraq's invasion and worried that Saddam might invade Saudi lands, he also believed that Saddam had been entrapped by the U.S., and enticed into invading Kuwait, by the United States.

Bin Laden, like Saddam, believed that the U.S. and Bush (senior) administration had given the Iraqi leader a "green light" to invade Kuwait. Given the subsequent harsh U.S. response, it seemed to bin Laden and others that the flip flop in U.S. policy was yet another Jewish inspired ploy to not only humiliate the Arab people but to destroy the only modern Arab country that posed a threat to Israeli dominance in the Middle East.

Bin Laden believed Saddam had been tricked into a self-destructive act that would justify the destruction of Iraq.

Bin Laden opposed Saddam's self-destructive foray into Kuwait and also opposed the massive transport of American troops to Islamic lands.

To bin Laden and other Islamic leaders, it now seemed clear that Saddam had been tricked into invading Kuwait, not only as a pretext to destroy Iraq, but as an excuse for the U.S. government to invade and occupy the Holy lands.

The U.S. was demanding that Kuwait, Yemen and Saudi Arabia allow American ground forces and American bases to be established on Arab lands in order to drive Saddam out of Kuwait.

These demands were violently opposed by bin Laden and other Arabs.

Bin Laden appealed to Arab leaders, including the Saudi leadership to rely on native fighters.

They listened and then acted otherwise.

Bin Laden, like millions of other Arabs, was outraged when the Saudi leadership turned Saudi Arabia over to the U.S. military.

Saudi Arabia, a small desert kingdom, is the home of Mecca—Islam's holiest of sites, and now the holy lands were invaded, not by Saddam, but by the American military.

Saudi Arabia, bin Laden's homeland, was overwhelmed by

more than half a million American troops—many of which were there to stay: Indefinitely.

This was sacrilege, an affront to god!

Worse, not only had the godless Americans invaded the Holy lands, but their women, female GIs, were prancing around "half naked," in shorts, revealing blouses and with their faces painted with rouge and makeup.

These actions were an insufferable insult to the pious, and bin Laden and others were enraged.

Female GIs, were soon ordered to dress more conservatively and to remain on base. But the damage was done.

The American infidels had arrived, bearing weapons, guns and innumerable gods. They had invaded the Holy lands. And they intended to stay.

As summed up by bin Laden: "For over seven years the United States has been occupying the lands of Islam in the holiest of places, the Arabian Peninsula, plundering its riches, dictating to its rulers, humiliating its people, terrorizing its neighbors and turning its bases in the Peninsula into a spearhead through which to fight the neighboring Muslim peoples."

Worse, although the American media made light of it, an incredible number of Arab men, women and children—over one million people, were killed by American-led forces during the Gulf War.

Adding insult to injury, the hundreds of thousands of civilian casualties were dismissed by the Bush administration as "collateral damage."

"Collateral damage."

From the perspective of bin Laden and millions of other Arabs, it appeared as if the U.S. did not even consider Arabs to be human beings. Dead Arabs, dead children, and dead women were simply "collateral damage."

Then there were the continuing anti-Arab policies of the Bush and Clinton administrations. Not only had the Iraqi people been vanquished, but the Muslims believed the U.S. now sought to punish the people of Iraq by imposing crippling economic sanctions—sanctions which destroyed the Iraqi economy and led to the death and mal-nourishment of hundreds of thousands of Iraqi children.

"Collateral damage."

As argued by bin Laden: "despite the great devastation inflicted on the Iraqi people by the crusader-Zionist alliance, and despite the huge number of those killed, which has exceeded 1 million... despite all this, the Americans are once against trying to repeat the horrific massacres, as they are not content with the protracted blockade imposed after the ferocious war or the fragmentation and devastation."

In the eyes of many Arabs, the American leaders were still killing Arab people and fully intended to continue killing Arab people.

Bin Laden: "If some people have in the past argued about the fact of the occupation, all the people of the Peninsula have now acknowledged it. The best proof of this is the Americans' continuing aggression against the Iraqi people using the Peninsula as a staging post, even though all its rulers are against their territories being used to that end, but they are helpless."

Worse, from the perspective of bin Laden, the U.S. was in fact participating in a massive campaign of massacre against Muslims all over the world.

As proclaimed by bin Laden in his declaration of holy war: "Muslim blood was spilled in Palestine and Iraq. The horrifying pictures of the massacre of Qana, in Lebanon are still fresh in our memory. Massacres in Tajakestan, Burma, Cashmere, Assam, Philippine, Fatani, Ogadin, Somalia, Erithria, Chechnia and in Bosnia-Herzegovina took place, massacres that send shivers in the body and shake the conscience. All of this and the world watched and heared and not only didn't respond to these atrocities, but also with a clear conspiracy between the USA and its' allies and under the cover of the iniquitous United Nations, the dispossessed people were even prevented from obtaining arms to defend themselves."

And why were Americans killing Arabs? Bin Laden and his allies believe the answer is clear: to serve Jewish-Zionist interests:

"So here they come to annihilate what is left of this people and to humiliate their Muslim neighbors. The Americans' aims behind these wars are religious and economic, the aim is also to serve the Jews' petty state and divert attention from its occupation of Jerusalem and murder of Muslims there. The best proof of this is their eagerness to destroy Iraq, the strongest neighboring Arab state and their endeavor to fragment all the states of the region such as Iraq, Saudi Arabia, Egypt and Sudan into paper statelets and through their disunion and weakness to guarantee Israel's survival and the continuation of the brutal crusade occupation of the Peninsula."

In the eyes and hearts of many Arabs, Americans had invaded the Holy lands, they were killing Muslims and the U.S. had declared war on all the Islamic people.

"All these crimes and sins committed by the Americans are a clear declaration of war on God, his messenger, and Muslims."

Bin Laden responded by declaring war on America:

"It is the individual duty for every Muslim to kill the Americans and their allies — civilians and military — it is an individual duty for every Muslim who can do it in any country in which it is possible to do it, in order to liberate the al-Aqsa Mosque and the holy mosque [Mecca] from their grip, and in order for their armies to move out of all the lands of Islam, defeated and unable to threaten any Muslim. This is in accordance with the words of Almighty God, 'and fight the pagans all together as they fight you all together,' and 'fight them until there is no more tumult or oppression, and there prevail justice and faith in God.'"

"We — with God's help — call on every Muslim who believes in God and wishes to be rewarded to comply with God's order to kill the Americans and plunder their money wherever and whenever they find it. We also call on Muslim ulema, leaders, youths, and soldiers to launch the raid on Satan's U.S. troops and the devil's supporters allying with them, and to displace those who are behind them so that they may learn a lesson."

"It is the duty of every Muslim to kill the Americans."

JIHAD: HOLY WAR
OSAMA BIN LADEN DECLARES HOLY WAR AGAINST THE "CRUSADER STATES OF AMERICA"

Bin Laden became a sworn enemy of the United States in 1991, the year of the Persian Gulf War.

The "American crusader forces" were "occupying" his homeland.

From the perspective of bin Laden and other pious Muslims, the intrusion of the "crusader forces" was a semblance to the days of the Christian led crusades of almost a thousand years before, during which the Catholic Church sought to evict the Muslims from the Holy lands.

It was thirteen hundred years ago, in the seventh century A.D., that the religion known as Islam arose in the Arabian peninsula. With astonishing rapidity, it quickly spread across and conquered the Middle East, Byzantium, Persia, northern Africa, and Spain.

Islam was spread by the sword.

The armies of the Christian Byzantine Empire were annihilated in 636, and Jerusalem fell in 638.

Four hundred years later, in the year 1095, the Catholic Pope Urban II proclaimed that war for the sake of God was holy. He called upon the nobility and their armies to go to forth and assist their Christian brothers, the Byzantines. and kill the Muslims in the name of God—a cause that could be justified by scripture:

"Behold I send an angel before thee, to keep thee in the way. Beware of him and obey his voice, for I will be an enemy unto thine enemies, and an adversary unto thine adversaries, and I will cut them off... I will send my terror before thee, and will destroy all the people to whom thou shalt come... and I will drive them out from before thee, until thou be increased and inherit the land."

—Exodus 23:20-30

However, it was not the pious that Urban desired to fight his wars, but lovers of murder and mayhem. He required killers to do a killer's job. He was interested in recruiting for his holy cause only those who were murderers, rapists, molesters of children and anyone who enjoyed the prolonged torture of their victims.

"You oppressors of orphans, you robbers of widows, you homicides, you blasphemers, you plunderers of others' rights... If you want to take counsel for your souls you must go forward boldly as knights of Christ..." so proclaimed the Pope who then offered "indulgences" and heavenly forgiveness to all those who would commit blasphemies and murder women and children in the name of the Lord God and Jesus Christ.

He had just launched the first crusade.

An important factor that played a role in helping to persuade the nobles and their armies to participate in such a gruesome task so terribly far from home, were the offers of an "indulgence."

An "indulgence" was literally a license to sin, to do harm, and it was a guarantee that all sins would be forgiven by god, no matter how odious the crime.

In consequence, the crusaders not only attacked and massacred the Muslims, successfully retaking Jerusalem on July 15, 1099, but they massacred their fellow Christians who had the misfortune and bad luck of living in villages that fell along the way—a pattern that was repeated in subsequent Crusades over the centuries.

For example, in the 13th century, an army of some thirty thousand Christian knights and Crusaders descended into southern France and attacked the town of Beziers in search of heretics. Over thirteen thousand Christians flocked to the churches for protection.

When the Bishop, one of the Pope's representatives, was informed that the army was unable to distinguish between true believers and heretics, he replied, "Kill them all. God will recognize his own."

******

The Muslims viewed the Christians as "polytheists," and idolaters, and set out to cleanse the Holy lands of these blasphemers.

The Islamic Holy Wars and Counter-Crusades began.

"In the Name of God... by the Troops shall the unbelievers be driven towards Hell, until when they reach it, its gates shall be opened... for just is the sentence of punishment on the unbelievers...."
—Koran, XXXIX

Saladin was the greatest of Muslim generals, and in 1187, he annihilated the entire army of the Kingdom of Jerusalem at the Horns of Hattin, near the Sea of Galilee. Jerusalem had again come under Islamic rule.

Now after nearly a thousand years, the "crusader forces" had returned and whereas the Medieval Catholic Church had been driven back and had failed to defeat the Muslim peoples, the United States had succeeded greatly. They had invaded the holiest of all Muslim lands, the land of Mecca, the Holy land of Saudi Arabia—which was an intolerable affront to 1,400 years of Islamic tradition. It was an afront to Allah, to god.

Over a thousand years ago, after driving out the polytheists and those who worshipped multiple gods and those who profaned the lands of Arabia, the prophet Muhammad had declared that hencefore there shall "not be two religions in Arabia."

Muhammad's words were law—he was the messenger of God.

And now, a thousand years later, the polythiests, the Crusaders had returned.

The presence of foreign troops, with their many gods, was blasphemous. It was a sin. It was a crime against god.

The American led, Western "crusader forces," of course, saw their presence in a whole different light. They were not the invaders. They were in Saudi Arabia to protect it from Saddam Hussein's armies and to liberate Kuwait.

From the perspective of the Americans, they were not an occupying force but remained stationed in Saudi Arabia after the Gulf War, in order to protect the kingdom from Saddam Hussein.

It was not just entirely on religious grounds that bin Laden and other Arabs were incensed. They also believed the presence of the "Crusader Forces" were corrupting the morals of the people and causing the kingdom of Saudi Arabia incredible economic and financial harm.

"The crusader forces became the main cause of our disastrous condition," he wrote in his 1996 declaration of jihad: Holy War.

******

In August of 1996, bin Laden formally declared war on the United States. The declaration of war and its justification was detailed in a document entitled, "Ladenese Epistle: Declaration of War."

He published this document in a London-based newspaper, Al Quds Al Arabi, which he had often used to communicate his views.

It read, in part, as follows:

DECLARATION OF WAR AGAINST THE AMERICANS OCCUPYING THE LAND OF THE TWO HOLY PLACES: EXPEL THE INFIDELS FROM THE ARAB PENINSULA

A MESSAGE FROM
USAMA BIN MUHAMMAD BIN IN LADEN

Praise be to Allah, we seek His help and ask for his pardon. we take refuge in Allah from our wrongs and bad deeds. Who ever has been guided by Allah will not be misled, and who ever has been misled, he will never be guided. I bear witness that there is no God except Allah, and I bear witness that Muhammad is His slave and messenger.

It should not be hidden from you that the people of Islam had suffered from aggression, iniquity and injustice imposed on them by the Zionist-Crusaders alliance and their collaborators; to the extent that the Muslims blood became the cheapest and their wealth as loot in the hands of the enemies. Their blood was spilled in Palestine and Iraq. The horrifying pictures of the massacre of Qana, in Lebanon are still fresh in our memory. Massacres in Tajakestan, Burma, Cashmere, Assam, Philippine, Fatani, Ogadin, Somalia, Erithria, Chechnia and in Bosnia-Herzegovina took place, massacres that send shivers in the body and shake the conscience. All of this and the world watch and hear, and not only didn't respond to these atrocities, but also with a clear conspiracy between the USA and its' allies and under the cover of the iniquitous United Nations, the dispossessed people were even prevented from obtaining arms to defend themselves.

The people of Islam awakened and understood that they were the main targets for the aggression of the Zionist-Crusaders alliance. All false claims and propaganda about "Human Rights" were hammered down and exposed by the massacres that took place against the Muslims in every part of the world.

The latest and the greatest of these aggressions, incurred by the Muslims since the death of the Prophet (ALLAH'S BLESSING AND SALUTATIONS ON HIM) is the occupation of the land of the two Holy Places -the foundation of the house of Islam, the place of the revelation, the source of the message and the place of the noble Ka'ba, the Qiblah of all Muslims- by the armies of the American Crusaders and their allies. (We bemoan this and can only say: "No power and power acquiring except through Allah").

The explosion at Riyadh and Al-Khobar is a warning of this volcanic eruption, which was emerging as a result of the severe oppression, suffering, excessive iniquity, humiliation and poverty.

People are fully concerned about their every day livings; everyone talks about the deterioration of the economy, inflation, increasing debts and jails full of prisoners. Government employees with limited income talk about debts of hundreds of thousands of Saudi Riyals. They complain that the value of the Riyal is greatly and steadily deteriorating among most of the main currencies. Great merchants and contractors speak about hundreds and thousands of million Riyals owed to them by the government. More than three hundred forty billions of Riyal owed by the government to the people in addition to the daily accumulated interest, let alone the foreign debt. People wonder and question whether we are the largest oil exporting country?! They even believe this situation is a curse put on them by Allah for not objecting to the oppressive and illegitimate behavior and measures of the ruling regime: Ignoring the divine Shari'ah law; depriving people of their legitimate rights; allowing the American to occupy the land of the two Holy Places; unjust imprisonment of the sincere scholars. The honorable Ulamah and scholars as well as merchants, economists and eminent people of the country were all alerted by this disastrous situation.

The inability of the regime to protect the country and allowing the enemy of the Ummah - the American crusader forces- to occupy the land for the longest of years. The crusader forces became the main cause of our disastrous condition, particularly in the economical aspect of it, due to the unjustified heavy spending on these forces. As a result of the policy imposed on the country, especially in the oil industry, where production is restricted or expanded and prices are fixed to suit the American economy and ignore the economy of the country. Expensive deals were imposed on the country to purchase arms. People questioning the justification of the existence of the regime.

Traitors implement the policy of the enemy in order to bleed the financial and the human resources of the Ummah, and leave the main enemy in the area-the American Zionist alliance enjoy peace and security! This is the policy of the American-Israeli alliance as they are the first to benefit from this situation.

But with the grace of Allah, the majority of the nation, both civilians and military individuals are aware of the wicked plan. They refused to be played against each other and to be used by the regime as a tool to carry out the policy of the American-Israeli alliance through their agent in our country: the Saudi regime.

If there are more than one duty to be carried out, then the most important one should receive priority. Clearly after Belief (Imaan) there is no more important duty than pushing the American enemy out of the holy land.

Ibn Taymiyyah, after mentioning the Moguls (Tatar) and their behavior in changing the law of Allah, stated that: the ultimate aim of pleasing Allah, raising His word, instituting His religion and obeying His messenger (ALLAH'S BLESSING AND SALUTATIONS ON HIM) is to fight the enemy, in every aspects and in a complete manner; if the danger to the religion from not fighting is greater than that of fighting, then it is a duty to fight them even if the intention of some of the fighter is not pure i.e. fighting for the sake of leadership (personal gain) or if they do not observe some of the rules and commandments of Islam. To repel the greater of the two dangers on the expense of the lesser one is an Islamic principle, which should be observed. It was the tradition of the people of the Sunnah (Ahlul-Sunnah) to join and invade- fight- with the righteous and non-righteous men. Allah may support this religion by righteous and non-righteous people as told by the prophet (ALLAH'S BLESSING AND SALUTATIONS ON HIM). If it is not possible to fight except with the help of non-righteous military personnel and commanders, then there are two possibilities: either fighting will be ignored and the others, who are the great danger to this life and religion, will take control; or to fight with the help of non righteous rulers and therefore repelling the greatest of the two dangers and implementing most, though not all, of the Islamic laws...."

******

In February of 1998, bin Laden published a second declaration of war: Ladenese Epistle.

OSAMA BIN LADEN DECLARES WAR (JIHAD) AGAINST JEWS & THE CRUSADERS

"Praise be to God, who revealed the Book, controls the clouds, defeats factionalism, and says in His Book: "But when the forbidden months are past, then fight and slay the pagans wherever ye find them, seize them, beleaguer them, and lie in wait for them in every stratagem (of war)"; and peace be upon our Prophet, Muhammad Bin-'Abdallah, who said: I have been sent with the sword between my hands to ensure that no one but God is worshipped, God who put my livelihood under the shadow of my spear and who inflicts humiliation and scorn on those who disobey my orders.

The Arabian Peninsula has never — since God made it flat, created its desert, and encircled it with seas — been stormed by any forces like the crusader armies spreading in it like locusts, eating its riches and wiping out its plantations. All this is happening at a time in which nations are attacking Muslims like people fighting over a plate of food. In the light of the grave situation and the lack of support, we and you are obliged to discuss current events, and we should all agree on how to settle the matter.

No one argues today about three facts that are known to everyone; we will list them, in order to remind everyone:

First, for over seven years the United States has been occupying the lands of Islam in the holiest of places, the Arabian Peninsula, plundering its riches, dictating to its rulers, humiliating its people, terrorizing its neighbors, and turning its bases in the Peninsula into a spearhead through which to fight the neighboring Muslim peoples.

If some people have in the past argued about the fact of the occupation, all the people of the Peninsula have now acknowledged it. The best proof of this is the Americans' continuing aggression against the Iraqi people using the Peninsula as a staging post, even though all its rulers are against their territories being used to that end, but they are helpless.

Despite the great devastation inflicted on the Iraqi people by the crusader-Zionist alliance, and despite the huge number of those killed, which has exceeded 1 million... despite all this, the Americans are once against trying to repeat the horrific massacres, as though they are not content with the protracted blockade imposed after the ferocious war or the fragmentation and devastation.

So here they come to annihilate what is left of this people and to humiliate their Muslim neighbors.

If the Americans' aims behind these wars are religious and economic, the aim is also to serve the Jews' petty state and divert attention from its occupation of Jerusalem and murder of Muslims there. The best proof of this is their eagerness to destroy Iraq, the strongest neighboring Arab state, and their endeavor to fragment all the states of the region such as Iraq, Saudi Arabia, Egypt and Sudan into paper statelets and through their disunion and weakness to guarantee Israel's survival and the continuation of the brutal crusade occupation of the Peninsula.

All these crimes and sins committed by the Americans are a clear declaration of war on God, his messenger and Muslims. And ulema have throughout Islamic history unanimously agreed that the jihad is an individual duty if the enemy destroys the Muslim countries. This was revealed by Imam Bin-Qadamah in "Al- Mughni," Imam al-Kisa'i in "Al-Bada'i," al-Qurtubi in his interpretation, and the shaykh of al-Islam in his books, where he said: "As for the fighting to repulse [an enemy], it is aimed at defending sanctity and religion, and it is a duty as agreed [by the ulema]. Nothing is more sacred than belief except repulsing an enemy who is attacking religion and life."

On that basis, and in compliance with God's order, we issue the following fatwa to all Muslims:

The ruling to kill the Americans and their allies — civilians and military — is an individual duty for every Muslim who can do it in any country in which it is possible to do it, in order to liberate the al-Aqsa Mosque and the holy mosque [Mecca] from their grip, and in order for their armies to move out of all the lands of Islam, defeated and unable to threaten any Muslim. This is in accordance with the words of Almighty God, "and fight the pagans all together as they fight you all together," and "fight them until there is no more tumult or oppression, and there prevail justice and faith in God."

This is in addition to the words of Almighty God: "And why should ye not fight in the cause of God and of those who, being weak, are ill-treated (and oppressed)? — women and children, whose cry is: 'Our Lord, rescue us from this town, whose people are oppressors; and raise for us from thee one who will help!'"

We — with God's help — call on every Muslim who believes in God and wishes to be rewarded to comply with God's order to kill the Americans and plunder their money wherever and whenever they find it. We also call on Muslim ulema, leaders, youths and soldiers to launch the raid on Satan's U.S. troops and the devil's supporters allying with them, and to displace those who are behind them so that they may learn a lesson.

Almighty God said: "O ye who believe, give your response to God and His Apostle, when He calleth you to that which will give you life. And know that God cometh between a man and his heart, and that it is He to whom ye shall all be gathered."

Almighty God also says: "O ye who believe, what is the matter with you, that when ye are asked to go forth in the cause of God, ye cling so heavily to the earth! Do ye prefer the life of this world to the hereafter? But little is the comfort of this life, as compared with the hereafter. Unless ye go forth, He will punish you with a grievous penalty, and put others in your place; but Him ye would not harm in the least. For God hath power over all things."

Almighty God also says: 'So lose no heart, nor fall into despair. For ye must gain mastery if ye are true in faith.'"

******

A few months after Osama bin Laden declared holy war on America, he was asked by an Arab journalist why had there been no immediate attacks to back up the threats?

"If we wanted to carry out small operations, it would have been easy to do," bin Laden replied. "The nature of the battle requires good preparation."

In the 1920s, Adolf Hitler, while languishing in the Lansburg prison fortress outside Munich, also wrote an epistle: "My Struggle."

Hitler explained in detail his grievances, the wrongs committed against Germany and the German people, how he would come to power, the tactics he would employ to gain power and what he would accomplish once power had been seized.

Hitler intended to make Germany the greatest military power the world had ever seen, he would drive out the Jews and then he would declare war on Eastern Europe and the Soviet Union.

He said what he would do, over and over again, in speeches, in newspaper articles, and in his book, Mein Kampf—and then he did it—much to the shock and surprise of French, British, American and Russian diplomats, presidents, prime ministers, dictators and kings.

Hitler later admitted he should never have published Mein Kampf; that he should have kept his plans secret.

Like Adolf Hitler, bin Laden has detailed his grievances, the wrongs he believes have been committed against the Muslim people, as well as his goals and the tactics he will utilize in achieving those goals.

He has said what he will do and he is acting on his threats—trying to make his nightmare vision a reality.

To Americans, his vision is truly nightmarish. But to the vast majority of Arabs, his views have enormous appeal. He offers not only hope and salvation but also vengeance and retribution.

During the 1700s, and the war for independence, the Americans waged successful guerilla campaigns in order to combat Britain's superior numbers and arms.

The Jews also employed guerrilla warfare, when they drove the British out of the Holy lands, during the 1940s.

Guerrilla warfare was also the preferred tactic of Fidel Castro in driving the American-backed Batista government from power in Cuba.

Again, the Viet Cong employed guerrilla warfare to drive the American invaders from Viet Nam.

Guerrilla warfare works. Terror is effective.

Terror and guerrilla warfare can even defeat a super power.

Bin laden embraces terror and guerrilla warfare as the most effective tool in fighting a more powerful enemy.

When Hitler came to power, he spent the next five years planning and preparing for war.

Bin Laden has also recognized the need for lengthy preparation.

Lengthy preparation and meticulous planning are his calling card—with many of his operations being in the planning and preparation stages for four or more years; and then he strikes.

In 1998, bin Laden announced his intentions to the world and the United States and called for the killing of "Americans and their allies, civilians and military . . . in any country in which it is possible to do it."

In 1998, U.S. targets were hit: the U.S. embassies in East Africa and the USS Cole in Aden, Yemen.

Years of planning went into the 1998 bomb attacks—just as bin Laden promised.

"The nature of the battle requires good preparation."

In 1998, he also promised that "the battle will inevitably move . . . to American soil."

In June of 2001, Osama bin Laden boasted that a horrific attack would soon take place in the United States.

On September 11, 2001, he made good on his terrorist threat. He murdered over 6,000 Americans.

******

The U.S. State Department believes that bin Laden's hydra-headed terrorist organization, al-Qa'eda, has over 3000 agents in over two dozen countries, including the United States.

Bin Laden has the resources and the international connections to successfully carry out an attack against American interests on almost any region of the globe.

Although headquartered in the remote mountains of Afghanistan, al-Qa'eda and bin Laden have agents in Albania, Algeria, Azerbaijan, Bangladesh, Bosnia, Canada, Chechnya, Ecuador, Egypt, Eritrea, Ethiopia, Jordan, Kenya, Kosovo, Lebanon, Libya, Malaysia, Mauritania, Pakistan, Philippines, Qatar, Saudi Arabia, Somalia, Sudan, Tajikistan, Tanzania, Tunisia, Uganda, United Kingdom, Uruguay, Uzbekistan, Yemen and most importantly the United States.

Bin Laden's terrorist organization, al-Qa'eda, has established paramilitary terror cells across the globe. It is one of the few non-governmental organizations with the reach, capability and funds to execute missions of mass murder and mayhem such as the September 11, 2001 terrorist attacks on America.

Bin Laden not only has the resources and the international connections, but he and his organization have been implicated in numerous well planned military and terrorist attacks on United States interests.

Although bin Laden did not formally declare war until 1996, his organization has been conducting terrorist attacks since 1991.

"The nature of the battle requires good preparation."

Good preparation, however, does not guarantee success.

In January 1995, members of al-Qa'eda planned to plant bombs on 11 U.S. jetliners. The intent was for the bombs to go off as these jets were flying over the Pacific. Fortunately the plot was discovered and foiled.

In 1998, he organized his first successful attack on American targets: The U.S. embassies in Dar es Salaam, Tanzania, and Nairobi, Kenya. Some 224 people died in the bombings of these two U.S. embassies.

Fazul Abdullah Mohammed, has been indicted by a U.S. District Court in New York for his alleged role in the bombing of the U.S. Embassy in Nairobi, Kenya. According to U.S, intelligence sources, he trained in Afghanistan with bin Laden.

American intelligence have also discovered that other attacks had been planned for the U.S. embassies in Uganda and Albania.

The Clinton administration retaliated against this brazen act of mass murder and the assaults on the U.S. embassies, by launching a series of Tomahawk cruise missiles to destroy bin Laden's camp in Afghanistan.

This attempt at retaliation was ineffective and financially taxing. A number of tents were destroyed and about 20 men, mostly Pakistani militants, were killed at a cost of 1 million dollars a missile. Bin Laden escaped.

The Clinton administration was also humiliated after destroying a milk formula factory in Sudan. Claims by his administration that the milk factory was producing biological weapons, were soon proved false. This was a propaganda coup for bin Laden and his allies, as they portrayed the missile attack on Sudan as an act of unjustifiable terror.

Two years later, bin Laden and al-Qa'eda tried to strike again. During the U.S. millennium celebrations, bin Laden's group planned to launch multiple terrorist strikes over multiple days. These plans however, were foiled when Ahmed Ressam, a native of Algeria, was caught when he entered the United States from Canada.

Ahmed Ressam was later convicted of attempting to plant explosives in key sites in the Los Angeles area. He later admitted he had been acting on orders received from bin Laden's organization.

Undaunted, Bin Laden's forces made yet another attack on October 2000. A small boat filled with explosives rammed the USS Cole as it was entering the harbor in Yemen.

Dozens of sailors were badly burned and injured. Seventeen were killed.

Soon after committing this dastardly deed, bin Laden filmed himself reciting a victory poem about the bombing of the Cole. He also issued a call to arms:

"To all the Mujah: Your brothers in Palestine are waiting for you; it's time to penetrate America and Israel and hit them where it hurts the most."

Osama bin Laden had issued his warning: He was preparing to strike hard at the hearts and minds of America.

******

"We were sitting in our office on the 86th floor. We have a wonderful view.

I was checking my e-mail, when Joe pointed toward the window and exclaimed "What the hell?"

It was a jet. A big Boeing. It was coming toward us... toward the towers... closer... faster... I could hear the scream of the engines... it was above us now and then... wham!

There was this tremendous jolt and an incredible explosion, which made our office rock back and forth. I was knocked off my feet. Book cases collapsed. Pictures fell off the walls. I could hear the building creaking as it swayed.

We lay there frozen, stunned.

Then, like confetti, all this stuff began falling past our windows... pieces of metal and concrete and glass... and then, oh my god—was that a woman!

Then the phone rang. It was surreal.

The lights were still on. The computers were still on. Yet all this stuff was still falling past our window... including, I couldn't believe it... another body...

"Let's get the hell out of here," I yelled, and we ran out into a fog of thick billowing black smoke.

Fire!

We tore off our shirts, wrapped them around our faces and ran to the stairwell. There were already people hurrying down, some of them badly burned... no hair, no eyebrows... their skin red and raw and smoking.

It was ghastly. And yet, everyone seemed so calm.

Down, down, down we went. But then we stopped.

Why were people coming back up? A door was locked.

There was no way down!

Some of the people started to panic. Women were crying.

The only way out would be to go back up and try another stairwell. — A Survivor

THE PLOT THICKENS: BIN LADEN'S FINGERPRINTS

The first attacks on America directly associated with bin Laden took place in Somalia, East Africa, Saudi Arabia and Yemen.

So far bin Laden had proved himself a minor irritant but a major embarrassment to the U.S. government.

True there had been deadly attacks against American targets, but the loss of American lives had proved to be few and far between. More importantly, none of the raids and incursions had occurred on American soil.

American officials were confident. A major strike would never happen here. We were inviolate, vigilant and prepared.

Although members of congress and administrative officials have given lip service to the threat posed by bin Laden, much of this was for public consumption.

The rhetoric was empty. Bin Laden was not being taken all that seriously. In fact, officials in the Bush administration even harbored the illusion that he, his supporters, and the Taliban government, which harbored him and provided him safe haven, could be bought off with a few million dollars.

In March of 2001, Colin Powell, the U.S. secretary of state, not only dangled a carrot worth over 40 million dollars to the rulers of Afghanistan—the same rulers that he and other administrative officials would partly blame for the September 11 attack, but he hand fed it to them, to the tune of $47 million dollars.

They took the money. They were all smiles.

Yet, again and again, bin Laden made it clear that he would bring his war to the American homeland. The battle will "inevitably move . . . to American soil," he said. "Our aim in life," he said, directing his words to American ears, "is to enter paradise by killing you."

A goodly portion of the 47 million dollars donated to the Afghan government most likely ended up in the bank accounts of bin Laden—funds which he used to finance the September 11 assault on the Pentagon and World Trade Center.

If this was a wakeup call, it was delivered with the power of a small atomic bomb—the killing power of a Boeing jet fully loaded with fuel.

******

Bin Laden has not only declared war on America, he and his followers believe they can win this war and can defeat a superpower and drive them from the Holy lands.

This attitude is not based on megalomania, but on experience.

In the 1980s, bin Laden and his merchants of mayhem, humbled and defeated the second greatest superpower on Earth: the Soviet Union.

With this victory, bin Laden and the mujaheddin demonstrated that a superpower can be defeated by a small and determined army. Bin Laden sent the Russians packing, with their tails between their legs.

Bin Laden and his associates believe America can also be easily defeated and driven from the Middle East and the Arabic Holy lands.

From his persepctive, this can only be accomplished through terror and by bringing the battle home to America.

He is confident he will prevail. He has promised that the horrific September 11 assault on America is just the beginning of a long protracted terror campaign.

In the future, bin Laden and his organization will attempt to plague U.S. with deadly diseases which his men shall deposit in the drinking water and dust upon the cities of America. In the future bin Laden and his men will destroy entire cities, with suitcase-sized nuclear bombs.

Bin Laden had declared war on America. The war will

continue until bin Laden and his men are buried and dead, or the U.S. capitulates and withdraws from the Holy land.

Bin Laden has also stated that he believes Americans will be easier to defeat than the Russians. The Russians, he has said, had to be beaten back and beaten again and again, and although the Russians fought with brutal tenacity and with superior arms, they were eventually chased from Afghanistan.

America, he believes, will be much easier to defeat and without the necessity of spilling so many thousands of gallons of Arab blood.

"The Russian soldier is more courageous and patient than the U.S. soldier," he told the London-based Arab newspaper, al-Quds al-Arabi. "Our battle with the United States will be easy compared with the battles in which we engaged in Afghanistan."

The best predictor of the future is the past, and in the past, terrorist attacks that have spilled large quantities of American blood, have resulted in the withdrawal of American forces.

Bin Laden bases this belief on the following: In 1983, America withdrew its military forces from Lebanon after the truck bombing of the Marine barracks in Beirut. Over 200 American men lost their lives.

In 1993, American forces withdrew from Somalia after the killings of 17 U.S. servicemen in Mogadishu.

In 2000, America withdrew many of its personnel from Yemen following the receipt of numerous terrorist threats and after the October attack on the USS Cole.

Bin Laden is media savvy and understands the use and the power of propaganda. In a video he produced, he bragged of the attack on the USS Cole.

"This big American ship... a destroyer" he later said, "had the illusion she could destroy anything... but was itself destroyed by a tiny boat...The destroyer represented the West, and the small boat represented Muhammad."

Bin Laden seeks to send a message to America and that message is of a nightmare world of terror... unceasing horror that will not end until America withdraws its forces from Islamic lands.

"Terrorism," he once said, "can be commendable... and reprehensible..."

"In today's wars there are no morals. Americans steal our wealth and our resources and our oil. Our religion is under attack. They kill and murder our brothers. They compromise our honor and our dignity and if we dare utter a single word of protest against the injustice, we are called terrorists."

Bin Laden believes that he is justified in killing innocent men and women, justified in burning them alive in a sea of flames, justified in murdering and maiming those who have never done him any harm, justified because he and his followers are waging a holy war against American "terrorism."

On September 11, 2001, war was declared on America.

******

The September 11 attacks on the Pentagon and the Twin Towers of the World Trade Center have bin Laden's fingerprints all over them. The attacks were meticulously planned with military precision and carried out by individuals directly linked to his organization.

Indeed, as recently as June of 2001, Osama bin Laden boasted of a horrific attack that would soon take place in the United States.

In the final days of August, Israel's Intelligence Agency, the Mossad, warned U.S. officials that as many as 200 terrorists linked to bin Laden had slipped into the country to prepare a major assault in the United States.

One of the best predictors of the future... is the past. And those who do not learn from the past, are condemned to re-experience it.

U.S. officials have known since 1993 that the World Trade Center was at the top of bin Laden's hit list for targets of terrorism.

Terrorists had previously attempted to bring down the World

Trade Center on February 26, 1993.

New York City and the Trade Center were targeted for several reasons. For one, New York is believed to be a "Jewish city."

Two, New York city and the World Trade Center were heavily populated. The World Trade Center was a city in-itself, with offices that could house over 50,000 people. If the World Trade Center could be destroyed, there would be an enormous and devastating loss of life--exactly what the terrorist most desires.

Three, New York is one of the most recognizable cities in the world. Four, the World Trade Center, the heartbeat of lower Manhattan, was viewed as a symbol of America's wealth.

The World Trade Center was an obvious target whose destruction would strike terror into the hearts of America, generate incredible publicity, and draw hundreds of new recruits eager to join a successful cause.

******

Mahmud Abouhalima, Mohammad Salameh, and Ramzi Yousef, spent months planning the first attack. They fashioned their bomb using $3,000 worth of common ingredients.

The bomb was loaded into a rented Ryder van and then transported from Jersey City, through the Holland Tunnel, into Manhattan. The van with its massive bomb ready to go off, was left in an underground parking garage beneath the World Trade Center.

The terrorists were convinced they were about to murder 50,000 Americans.

Then they ran.

Yousef didn't remain in New York to savor the "triumph." He immediately grabbed a flight at John F. Kennedy Airport, flew to Frankfurt Germany and then made his way to Afghanistan—the home base of bin Laden.

Abouhalima was too excited to flee. Instead he went to Tower Records in downtown Manhattan and waited patiently in the classical music section for the apocalypse.

Mohammad Salameh also waited and watched.

And then, the bomb exploded.

Although the World Trade Center shook and trembled, it did not collapse.

Although thousands were injured, only six people were killed.

The terrorists were angered and embittered.

They had failed.

Mohammad Salameh was so disgusted by the results, he felt so cheated, that he disobeyed orders from his group and returned to the Ryder truck rental office in Jersey City.

He wanted his money back.

He demanded that his deposit on the van be returned.

He was immediately arrested.

Two years later, master terrorist Ramzi Yousef who had helped to plan the bombing, was also apprehended.

Following his capture, when FBI agents flew fugitive Ramzi Yousef back to New York to face justice, he glanced down at the World Trade Center and frowned.

"See," an FBI agent said as he pointed out the twin skyscrapers from the helicopter. "The Twin Towers are still standing."

Yousef replied, "They wouldn't be if I had enough money and explosives."

Bin Laden had drawn the same conclusions: Enough money and explosive power could transform Yousef's cataclysmic dream into a nightmare reality.

Bin Laden and his organization began to plot.

Eight years later, on September 11, 2001, hell would rain from the skies. Two fuel laden jetliners enroute from Boston to Los Angeles were hijacked and then hammered into the Trade Center, collapsing the New York landmark and altering the lives of Americans forever.

Less than an hour later, another aircraft, which had departed from Washington's Dulles Airport, would become a guided missile aimed at the heart of American's military might, the Pentagon.

******

"I stepped out onto the sidewalk and stood there dazed, in shock, my eyes transfixed on the scene of utter horror above me.

Then I realized there were people all around who were badly hurt, who had been struck by the falling glass, shards of bent steal, and concrete.

A young woman in pearls, high heels and a short dark skirt lay on the street, blood flowing from her head.

And there was a man, in a three-piece suit, leaning in a twisted, impossible angle, with blood seeping out of his chest, forming a dribbling crimson pool on the sidewalk.

Another man rushed passed me... he had been slashed and stabbed by falling glass.

People were running, screaming, crying... but there were also others, like me, who just stood there in shock.

And when I looked up, again, there were people jumping and falling falling...

It was like a bad dream... a nightmare...

I couldn't stand it. I began to run.

— *A Survivor*

"I had been late for work and was hurrying from the sub-way to the World Trade Center.

Suddenly the sky exploded...then it began raining glass and bits of concrete... and... and body parts... There were body parts everywhere...

And jumpers. Tons of them.

People jumping and falling who were on fire... burning alive... It was surreal.

Every time you looked up somebody else was jumping.

You could see person after person going straight down, no floating or anything.

It was the sickest thing I've ever seen in my whole life..."

— *A Survivor*

WAS ANYBODY LISTENING?

In the mountains of Afghanistan, in safe houses in Germany and Canada, and in cities scattered in Florida, California and Massachusetts, the hijackers prepared for the coming apocalypse that would engulf the citizens of America and collapse the Twin Towers of the World Trade Center.

The attack was directed from bin Laden's terrorist camps in Afghanistan, planned with military precision, and would involve agents and operatives on three continents.

******

The operation was meticulously planned and ingeniously carried out.

Terrorists, recruiters, fund raisers, and spies were planted in communities across America.

They lived among us.

The Kamikazi suicide pilots received flight training in Florida.

They were trained in the United States.

Detailed studies of the power of airline fuel were conducted, fuel consumption analyzed and airport security was repeatedly tested and concluded to be easily penetrable.

And, from previous hijackings it was already well known that airline pilots were specifically trained to fully cooperate with hijackers.

It was a bold, audacious, fine tuned, amazingly well coordinated, malicious operation.

The core attack team included 19 men. They were mostly Saudis and Egyptians.

Many of the hijackers appear to have been members of the

Islamic Jihad and al-Gamaa al-Islamiya—the central core of bin Laden's Praetorian Guard in the internationally based al-Qa'eda.

Several of these men were veterans of previous terrorist attacks. Mohamed Atta may have participated in a previous attack in Israel. Two of the hijackers, Salem Alhamzi and Khalid Al-Midhar were on a special terrorist-watch list given to Border Patrol and INS agents on August 21, 2001.

There were excellent reasons for keeping an eye on Khalid Al-Midhar and to keep him out of the country. The year before he had been videotaped meeting with one of the suspects in the Oct. 12, 2000 terrorist attack of the USS Cole.

Khalid Al-Midhar had no difficulty entering the United States.

Borders agents, the INS and the FBI were caught napping.

Although the INS and Border Patrol had been alerted, Khalid Al-Midhar, a man known to have been associating with known terrorists, legally entered the United States on a business visa.

Salem Alhamzi also waltzed freely right in and did so in a legal manner. He had a business visa.

Despite the fact that both were considered dangerous, they were allowed free entry into the U.S., and immediately set up housekeeping together at the "Marriott Hotel" in New York, which was listed as their official residence.

On September 11, Khalid Al-Midha and Salem Alhamzi would hijack American Airlines flight 77 and then crash it into the Pentagon.

Another hijacker, Mohamed Atta, 33, had also been implicated in previous terrorists attacks and earlier in the year he had met with a senior Iraqi intelligence officer.

Atta and another hijacker, his "cousin" Marwan, had also been linked by German authorities to Islamic extremists and the bin Laden organization.

And yet, although by law neither man should have been issued visas, both were granted visas and legally entered the country together. They immediately established a residence in Florida.

There they received extensive pilot training.

On September 11, Atta would hijack American Airlines Flight 11, and Marwan Flight United Airlines Flight 175. The two "cousins" who should have never been allowed to enter the United States, and who received pilot training in the United States, would each barrel their commandeered planes, Kamikaze style into the north and south Towers of the World Trade Center.

******

The attack, brilliant in its conception, would be years in planning. When carried out, the operation would be audacious, incredibly well coordinated and diabolical in its execution. It would be a spectacular triumph unequaled in the world of terrorism.

Bin Laden had repeatedly promised to bring his holy war to the shores of the United States. Bin Laden had also begun bragging early last year that he was about to launch major attacks on the United States, unlike anything the world had seen before.

Additional warnings would come in the months, weeks, and yes, even in the days immediately preceding the unparalleled assaults on America.

In December of 1999, an Algerian terrorist, Ahmed Ressam, was apprehended at the U.S.-Canadian border.

Ressam had orders to assist in the bombing of Los Angeles International Airport during the millennium celebrations.

The plot was defeated when Ressam was caught trying to enter Washington state from Canada in a car loaded with explosives.

Ressam was linked to bin laden.

Ressam took his orders from Haydar Abu Doha, who had close ties to bin Laden. Haydar Abu Doha, who was arrested recently on terrorism conspiracy charges, is a key figure in bin Laden's network.

According to Federal prosecutors, in 1998, Haydar Abu Doha met with bin Laden in Afghanistan. The purpose of these meetings was "to discuss cooperation and coordination between al-Qa'eda and a group of Algerian terrorists whose activities Abu Doha coordinated and oversaw."

Ressam was later provided a skeletal briefing of what was discussed in Afghanistan. Bin Laden's organization, al-Qa'eda was planning to carry out coordinated terrorist assaults on high profile American targets.

Ressam was to take an active part in these attacks. He had also journeyed to Afghanistan to receive special training.

As part of a plea bargain, Ahmed agreed to provide FBI agents with details.

The special training he received in bin Laden's camps included urban warfare, assassination, sabotage, hijacking and the destruction of the U.S. infrastructure. Targets included airports, airlines, the financial markets, New York City, Washington DC., the White House and the Pentagon. American airports and commercial jetliners would be used as weapons in the attack.

Bin Laden, he warned, would soon unleash an incomprehensible horror on the people of the United States.

The FBI, the CIA and U.S. intelligence agencies did not take him seriously.

In August of 2001, Israeli intelligence services, including the Mossad, became aware that Osama bin Laden was planning a large-scale terror attack on America, though they did not know exactly what or where his targets would be.

The Los Angeles Times subsequently discovered that Israel's Mossad had passed on warnings to U.S. officials that as many as 200 terrorists linked to bin Laden had slipped into the country and were preparing to launch a major assault on the United States.

"Everybody knew about a heightened alert, and knew that bin Laden was preparing a big attack," admitted an administration official on conditions of anonymity.

When asked by reporters if it was true that Israel had shared this frightening information with U.S. intelligence agencies, Mark Regev, Israel's ambassador to the United States admitted that:

"Israel routinely shares with the U.S. intelligence information concerning the field of counter terrorism. We also have been closely watching bin Laden and people were aware of the threat he poses."

After the September 11 assault, when confronted by newspaper reporters about this startling revelation, the CIA officially denied receiving advance warning: "That is utter nonsense," responded Bill Harlow, CIA spokesman.

CIA denials were seconded by senior Israeli government officials: "There was no specific information about the intention to carry out such an attack," the official said.

Even more astounding, during the first days of September, 2001, a little over a week before the September 11 attack, an Iranian awaiting deportation from Germany and seeking asylum in America, relayed a warning to United States security agencies, including the CIA and the White House. He warned that in about one week, bin Laden would launch a horrific terrorist attack on America, more nightmarish than the world has ever seen.

He made 14 other calls to the American authorities in the days immediately before the attack.

The FBI dismissed his warnings as lacking credibility.

The warnings were not taken seriously.

Even the warnings delivered by bin Laden were not taken seriously.

A reporter with ties to bin Laden informed U.S. officials that an attack was eminent. Bin Laden had been boasting that a horrific assault would soon be launched against the United States.

The FBI, the CIA and Bush administration officials knew that the number one target for a terrorist attack was the World Trade Center. The World Trade Center had been struck in 1993. One of the best predictors of the future, is the past... and yet, these warnings were not taken seriously.

Were U.S. intelligence officials just giving lip service to the war on terrorism?

In May of 2001, Bush announced that Vice President Dick

Cheney would lead a task force in reviewing programs to protect the United States from "the threat of weapons of mass destruction."

Bush also announced the creation of an Office of National Preparedness to deal with terrorist attacks.

But the Cheney task force made little if any progress.

Also bogged down was the establishment of the Preparedness Office. The fight against terrorism fell victim to bureaucratic infighting between the Department of Justice and the Federal Emergency Management Agency.

Politics and the lust for power took precedence over protecting the American people against the likes of Osama bin Laden.

The "task force" to fight terrorism was leaderless, rudderless, and had become essentially deaf and dumb to the accumulating evidence, including warnings from leaders in congress, that the U.S. was at risk for a major terrorist attack.

But what of the CIA, the FBI, the National Security Agency and the numerous other government organizations whose mission is to ferret out information on terrorist attacks in order to protect the citizens of this country? Why were they so unprepared?

Or were they?

The evidence that something was up, the signs that the repeatedly promised, upcoming attack was in play, were everywhere.

Individuals known or suspected to be linked with bin Laden or other terrorists groups, had been slipping into the country. Individuals who were being watched, who were on the FBI's "watch list" were holding late night meetings that were attended by other men who were being watched, and many of these men then attended yet other meetings at different locations with yet other men on the FBI's "watch list."

In fact, a dozen different individuals that the FBI maintains on a "watch list" and who are or were under some form of surveillance, not only met together, but shared the same U.S. addressees. Many of those on the "watch list" had also been living with several of the hijackers.

Specifically, eight of those on the FBI's watch list lived at the same address as two of the hijackers Hamza Alghamdi and Ahmed Alghamdi. Hamza and Ahmed were on the jet that hit the South Tower of the World Trade Center.

These eight men, were all under surveillance, were all living together and all sharing a dormitory at Flight Safety International-a flight school in Vero Beach. They were training to be pilots. They had no interest in learning how to take off or land.

The FBI did not consider that suspicious.

The FBI had been warned of a major bin Laden terrorist attack which would involve commercial jetliners and commercial airports. Six of those on the watch list were pilots certified by the Federal Aviation Administration.

The FBI again, was not suspicious.

Yet another certified pilot on the FBI's watch list shared an address in Daytona Beach with Waleed Alshehri, a hijacker on the flight that struck the north Tower of the World Trade Center. Also at that address: Saeed Alghamdi, a hijacker on the flight that crashed in Pennsylvania.

Waleed Alshehri and his brother Wail Alshehri, also shared yet another address with a woman living in Hollywood, Florida, also named on the "watch list." And, she shared their surname: Alshehri.

A Coral Springs man who was also on the FBI's watch list shared the same address as Marwan Al-Shehhi and Mohamed Atta both of whom participated in the hijackings. Mohamed Atta had also been implicated in previous terrorist attacks, and earlier in the year he had met with a senior Iraqi intelligence officer. Atta, had also been linked to bin Laden.

And yet, although a man suspected of terrorist activities was sharing an address with two men with known terrorist connections—two men who should not have even been allowed into this country—the FBI was still not suspicious.

Even more astounding, 18 men on the FBI's watch list lived

in the Vero Beach area, minutes away from the others, and these men too were pilots or undergoing flight training. And, they frequently met together late at night.

To summarize, five of these men end up living together at one address and eight others at a second address. They lived only a few miles away from each other. A total of 18 men on the "watch list," would frequently meet with one another late at night at different residences.

Most of these individuals were undergoing flight training, or were already pilots, or associating with those receiving pilot training.

And, the FBI did not become suspicious.

In addition, several of those on the FBI's watch list, were associating with a known terrorist and with two more men with links to bin Laden. All are studying to become pilots or are already pilots, yet the U.S. intelligence officials who were supposed to be watching them, never became suspicious?

These people were on a "watch list." They were supposed to be "watched." Their activities and those they associated with were supposed to be duly noted and if remotely suspicious, they were to be reported, investigated and checked out.

Didn't happen.

The FBI says its not their fault. They need more expensive computers.

But, if the FBI agent running those computers doesn't have the brains to become suspicious, then what good are the computers?

In fact, not only were almost all of the hijackers associating with those on the "watch list, but two of them, Atta and Marwan by law, should have never been granted visas or allowed into the country. Both were linked by German authorities to Islamic extremists and the bin Laden organization. Atta was suspected of involvement in the 1986 terrorist attack in Israel.

Bin Laden's operation has also been under constant surveillance.

As reported by Bob Woodward and Vernon Loeb in the Washington Post: "The CIA has been authorized since 1998 to use covert means to disrupt and preempt terrorist operations planned abroad by Saudi extremist Osama bin Laden under a directive signed by President Bill Clinton and reaffirmed by President Bush this year, according to government sources."

And yet, although they had been repeatedly warned, although known terrorists and those closely linked with terrorist organizations were streaming into the country, although men on the FBI's watch list were training to become pilots and were holding late night meetings, the Bush administration and U.S. intelligence agencies were caught with their pants down. It was not a pretty sight.

From the perspective of many in the intelligence community, the failure to detect and circumvent the attack on America, the failure to take seriously the numerous reports of an eminent massive attack, is not just inexcusable but is evidence of gross incompetence at the highest levels of the U.S. Government.

In fact, some have argued the behavior of the U.S. government was criminally negligent and that they too have blood on their hands...the blood of the thousands who died in the Twin Towers of the World Trade Center and the blood of those who died trying to save them.

After the September 11, attack, Robert S. Mueller III, Director of the FBI, said he was surprised to discover there were terrorists in the U.S., and even more surprised to learn they had been receiving flight training.

"This is news to me" he said, and then added, "obviously, if we had understood that to be the case, we would have averted this."

The FBI didn't know?

This was "news?"

In 1996 the FBI learned that Abdul Hakim Murad and two other men, had received flight training at four different flight schools in the U.S. during the early 1990s: Coastal Aviation,

Richmor Aviation, Schenectady flight school and Alpha Tango Flying Services in San Antonio. Murad was subsequently convicted of plotting to crash a suicide plane into CIA headquarters and blow up a dozen U.S. commercial jetliners over the Pacific.

Moreover, Murad was recruited by Ramzi Ahmed Yousef, a bin Laden operative. This is the same Ahmed Yousef who had plotted and carried out the 1993 World Trade Center bombing.

Specifically, in addition to the World Trace Center bombing, it was determined in 1996, that Yousef and Murad had been plotting to train and deploy five-man terrorist teams who were to infiltrate and bomb 12 different commercial jetliners, including Northwest Airlines, Delta Air Lines, and United Airlines. U.S. government prosecutors described the plot as "one of the most hideous crimes anyone ever conceived.".

In 1996, the FBI again received information that Arab pilots were plotting with Pakistani terrorists to plant bombs on a number of U.S. airliners.

In 1998, there was evidence that terrorists trained as pilots were planning an attack on the U.S.

Numerous references to pilot training and flight schools were discovered in documents uncovered during the investigation of the terrorists who had committed the 1998 bombings of U.S. embassies in Kenya and Tanzania.

Two participants in the 1998 bombings, who subsequently turned government informant, also informed the FBI that they and other men directly linked with bin Laden had received pilot training.

For example, Essam al-Ridi, had taken classes at the Ed Boardman Aviation School in Fort Worth. L'Houssaine Kerchtou, admitted that bin Laden had sent him to a flight school in Nairobi.

In addition, the FBI learned that one of bin Laden's associates, Ihab Ali Nawawi, received flight training at Airman Flight School in Norman, Oklahoma. This same Ihab Ali Nawawi was linked to the 1998 embassy bombings.

The FBI and the CIA had known for years that men associated with Osama bin Laden were in the United States. They knew for years that these men were receiving pilot training at U.S. schools in the United States. They were in fact aware that over a dozen people with links to bin Laden and his organization were attending U.S. flight schools.

Moreover, they not only received warnings in the days before the attack from an Iranian, but in late August, just weeks before the attack they received a warning from Managers of the International Flight School in Eagan, Minnesota about an Arab who requested training in a Boeing 747 simulator.

Why did the flight instructors consider this suspicious?

The Arab only wanted to learn how to steer the jet and had no interest in learning about landings or takeoffs. "He just wanted to learn to steer the plane, which was very odd."

It turned out that this "odd" man, Zacarias Moussaoui, had already been arrested on August 17, four weeks before the attacks. The FBI was contacted soon after his arrest by French intelligence and informed that Zacarias Moussaoui was a suspected terrorist and a fanatical believer in Islam.

Although a flight instructor considered it odd that an Arab had no interest in learning how to land and take off, only steer, the FBI did not consider this suspicious.

Despite the overwhelming evidence pointing directly to the obvious, it never occurred to anyone in the FBI or the Clinton or Bush administration that these men were learning how to fly in order to hijack planes and carry out ghastly suicide attacks.

"We were unable to marry any information from investigations or the intelligence community that talked to their use of this expertise in the events that we saw unfold on the 11th," an administration official said.

SO MANY TERRORISTS: SO LITTLE TIME

U.S. intelligence agencies have foiled numerous terrorist plots, including the plan to bomb targets in the United States and the Middle East on New Year's Day last year.

"Many terrorism cells have been rolled up in many countries, and this has often been done quietly," said Daniel Benjamin, who worked in the Clinton White House.

In 1992, the CIA foiled a plot by bin Laden agents to purchase highly enriched uranium from the "Russian Black Market."

Again, in 1993, the CIA working in conjunction with Russian intelligence agents uncovered a plot by bin Laden associates to buy radioactive materials and "suit case nukes"—nuclear bombs small enough to fit in a suitcase. They had been seeking to purchase these bombs from Chechen rebels.

Russian General Alexander Lebed, later admitted, however, that 43 "suitcase nukes" had nevertheless disappeared and could not be accounted for.

In September of 1998, the CIA and FBI, in a joint operation, prevented associates of bin Laden from obtaining nuclear materials. Mamdough Mahmud Salim, an aide to Bin Laden, had been negotiating to purchase $1.5 million dollars worth of high-grade uranium, and, a "suitcase nuclear bomb." He was arrested in Munich, Germany.

"Unfortunately, if just one conspiracy succeeds," Daniel Benjamin continued, "it looks as if America has fallen down on the job."

******

The FBI says it needs more expensive computers if the U.S. hopes to foil future attacks on American soil.

Others have argued that what is needed is diligence and just plain old common sense.

The problem with "common sense" is that it is not all that common.

Yet another problem is that even if a plot is foiled and the agents of destruction are arrested, there are plenty of others who are willing to step forward and assume their place.

Often the men directly responsible for the attack have only been told enough in order to accomplish their aspect of the mission. If one agent is stopped or killed, the mission may go forward, or, the others may regroup and wait for the next order to begin the attack.

Bin Laden's terrorist organization consists of cells, or battle groups that are only pieces of a larger system. Together they constitute a network of semi-independent operatives and agents, which include: recruiters, teachers, trainers, clerics, suicide bombers, technical advisers, bankers, and so on.

Even many of the men working within the same terrorist battle group do not know each other and do not know the identity of the person they are communicating with, or the person in charge of the operation.

These plotters have a lot of different operatives on the ground unaware of the plan's intricate details.

Those in charge, or their lieutenants, might also rely on local people to do the scout work, so that even if one or two are caught it is difficult for government intelligence to piece together the entire plot.

Agents may be ordered to carry out a task but have no idea why, or even from whom the orders came from. In this way, even if the members of a particular terrorist cell are captured, the plot can still move forward.

"If you compromise one cell, you don't take down the entire organization," said Frank Cilluffo, a policy analyst at the

Center for Strategic and International Studies.

Terrorism is hydra-headed. If an arm or a leg happens to be chopped off, another one will replace it.

"When these people are captured... or when a suicide bomber kills himself, there are other volunteers to take their place," said Vincent Cannistraro, former chief of counter-terrorism at the CIA.

There are hundreds of young men who would readily die for Islam and to achieve martyrdom.

******

Members of the U.S. Congress are now pushing to make assassination legal and to use it as a weapon against terrorism. Bin Laden would be the number one target on the assassination hit list.

Unfortunately, assassination is not really a viable option. Bin Laden moves about in secrecy and has innumerable hideouts.

"We just don't have the kind of intelligence on bin Laden we need to guarantee a successful mission," says Paul Bremer, former U.S. ambassador for counter-terrorism during the Reagan administration. "You can't go on yesterday's information."

Even if bin Laden was assassinated, the U.S. would remain subject to terrorist attacks carried out by his followers, or other independent terrorist organizations.

He may also be more dangerous dead than alive.

In death he would also become a powerful symbol: A martyr.

His followers would retaliate and perhaps even more young men would step forward to join his cause and to emulate his example: To die for Islam and to become a martyr.

Recognizing the inevitability of his own death, perhaps by assassination, bin Laden already has contingency plans in place, in case he is killed or captured.

Bin Laden has assigned the leading leadership positions in his organization, al-Qa'eda, to his two top deputies: Muhammad AteAyman, and al-Zawahiri,

Al-Zawahiri, is a physician and leader of an Egyptian terrorist group, al-Jihad. In 1995, al-Jihad massacred 62 people, many of them tourists, in Luxor, Egypt.

AteAyman and al-Zawahiri are believed to have played major roles in the planning and execution of the attacks on the USS Cole in the Yemeni port of Aden, and the 1998 U.S. Embassy bombings in East Africa. Both were also likely major players in the September 11 kamikaze attacks on the Pentagon and the Twin Towers of the World Trade Center.

"Muhammed AteAyman and al-Zawahiri are the tactical men responsible for the day-to-day operations," says terrorism expert Neil Livingstone, CEO of GlobalOptions, a Washington-based crisis-management company. "You can't take out a bin Laden and think that's the magical solution. He's got his team in place."

As summed up by Secretary of State Colin Powell: "Even if we were to get Osama bin Laden tomorrow —or if he was turned over to us— that would be good, but it would not be the end. It's his lieutenants we have to get. It's the whole network that has to be ripped up. We can't take out the head and have the tail and other parts laying around."

Yet another major problem in fighting terrorism is that there are so many plotters and dozens of terrorists groups, all of which share a fanatical hatred for the United States.

Bin Laden and his team, are not the only terrorist game in town.

Even wiping out his entire terrorist network would not stop deadly terrorist attacks on innocent people. The legacy of his organization would spawn other terrorist groups. And, there are already hundreds of terrorist organizations that would easily and happily fill the void, including those who completely shun publicity and prefer to remain hidden in the shadows.

The list of significant terrorism players in the world include:

Ayman Zawahiri, the leader of the Egyptian Islamic Jihad. Zawahiri was convicted in absentia and sentenced to death for the 1981 assassination of Egypt's President Anwar Sadat. Ayman Zawahiri has often appeared side by side with bin Laden.

Then there is "Abu Zubaydah" or Mohammed Hussein Zein-al-Abideen, a Palestinian who hails from Gaza. At one time, Abu Zubaydah worked as bin Laden's chief executive officer. He served as a key contact for several terrorist cells operating out of Western Europe and the Balkans in the 1990s.

The Armed Islamic Group in Algeria, another terrorist group with ties to bin Laden, hijacked an Air France plane on Christmas Eve 1994. The terrorists intended to blow it up over Paris. The plane got as far as Marseille, where it stopped for refueling. Fortunately, it was stormed by French commandos, and the passengers freed. Still, three people were killed.

******

So many terrorists, so little time to stop them. It is nearly impossible to keep track of the major players in the world of terrorism.

What makes the task of keeping track and foiling plots even more difficult is that many of the organizations do not work together, and many work against each other. Even those who have the same goals, such as the toppling of America as a military and financial superpower, generally do not cooperate and do not trust one another.

Bin Laden and his organization are just one among many.

According to Richard Murphy, a former U.S. ambassador to Saudi Arabia and Syria and who presently serves on the Council on Foreign Relations: "There are a whole flock of organizations that don't necessarily follow bin Laden's orders. Many terrorist organizations have never even had contact with him."

Bin Laden, however, is probably America's most dangerous adversary in the world of terrorism. All eyes should be trained and focused on bin Laden, because he and his organization are growing like a cancer. His tentacles stretch throughout the world, even reaching into the private homes of those living in the United States.

Because of his wealth and especially his fame, new recruits are easy to attract. In Pakistan and other Arabic countries, T-shirts and turbans bearing the image of Osama bin Laden are popular items.

In the open markets you can purchase fake $50 bills with his picture and the phrase "In Osama We Trust."

Colorful posters with his image and the words: "World Hero" are hot items and quickly sell out.

His cassettes and CDs in which he teaches that "Every American man is my enemy," are best sellers.

"Osama has become like a god for the Muslim people," said Kamal Hussein, 23. "America should be warned: American blood will flow in the streets."

The followers of Osama, the god, and those who wish to join his movement, do so for many reasons: Hatred of the United States. Hatred of Israel. But also because association with bin Laden offers prestige and power.

The large pools of disenfranchised, unemployed young adults who view the United States and Israel with outrage, anger and hate, are willing converts to his movement, particularly in that his rhetoric is delivered with all the fire and brimstone of a fundamentalist evangelist. His is a religious movement. And America is the Great Satan.

"A typical candidate is a young man from a religious home, first approached in the mosque, then recruited, tested and trained to be a walking bomb," says terrorism expert Brian Jenkins. "They are acting in their view with the approval of God."

And yet, the Koran, the Islamic holy book, forbids suicide. Most Moslem clerics condemn the suicide bombers.

Yet many others see suicide by bombing to be a heroic act. Some applaud because they wish a taste of the sweet wine of revenge.

In addition to those with a deep commitment to God, re-cruiters also seek out desperate young men drowning in a sea of poverty, hopelessness and despair.

A 19-year-old Palestinian Samir Toubasi, who was apprehended with a 22-pound bomb strapped to his back outside an Israeli disco, was asked why would he want to kill himself and so many young Israelis?

"I lost my job, my future, my hope. Then Israeli soldiers killed my friend. I too wanted to die."

Samir Toubasi didn't want his death to be in vein. He wanted to make a difference. He wanted to do something for his people. He also wanted revenge.

In Israel, Palestinian men who are taken into custody are often tortured by the authorities. As acknowledged by the U.S. State Department, although Israel is a democracy, Arabs living in Israel, are treated as second class citizens. Racism is rampant. Arabs are often beaten and attacked by Jews and the police are reluctant or unwilling to protect them—even though these Arabs are Israeli citizens. During one recent peaceful demonstration, the Israeli police fired into a crowd of 300 Arab citizens of Israel who were protesting peacefully. Dozens were seriously wounded and many killed.

In Israel, Jews convicted of the cold blooded murder of Arab-Israeli citizens, or Palestinian guest workers, might receive a sentence of 18 months in jail.

It is Israel government policy to assassinate Palestinian men "suspected" of orchestrating terror attacks. There are no courts, lawyers or trials, just summary judgements: execution.

The Israelis use bombs, missiles, tanks and helicopter gun ships to carry out assassinations with little or no concern for "collateral damage" i.e. the killing of innocent civilians and Arab women and children who may be in the same vehicle, building or room.

Arabs view these acts as cowardly declarations of war. In their view, Arabs are willing to die for their cause. Israelis hide behind billion-dollar American-made weaponry, which can kill easily from a safe distance.

And every death, every injury at the hands of the Israeli authorities, fuels and sets the spark of Arab rage. And this rage is directed not just at Israel, but against America, Israel's chief ally.

Israel frequently calls upon America to provide logistical support in their war against Islamic extremists and help ferreting out those who will be targeted for assassination. America has always obliged.

From the perspective of the Arab extremists, terrorists and "freedom fighters," America has Arab blood on its hands. America and Israel are therefore legitimate targets for terror.

******

Then there is the "occupation" of the holy lands in Saudi Arabia—another outrage from the perspective of many Arabs.

Then there are the crippling sanctions imposed against Iraq—another outrage from the perspective of many Arabs.

From the Arab percepive, so long as America continues to blindly support Israel, so long as U.S. troops remain in the Middle East and so long as there is poverty and hopelessness, then there will be young men who are willing to not only join in the "holy war" against America and Israel, but to die fighting that war even if it means killing innocent women and children—sometimes especially it if means the slaughter of the innocents.

THE MONEY TRAIL

"Money is the root of all evil."

With every successful terrorist operation, such as the September 11 assault on the pride of America, more and more "freedom fighters" flock to the doors of terrorism and beg entry. Bin Ladin's prestige, becomes their prestige. They see themselves as joining a winning and unified team.

And many of those who wish to join his ranks or share in the glory, come bearing gifts: Money. Lots of money.

Because of his power and prestige, other terrorists groups also actively seek his support and his blessing.

Prior to bin Laden, most terrorist organizations, if they wanted to engage in high-impact terrorism, had to seek funding and resources from outlaw nation-states. Bin Laden makes that unnecessary. He is incredibly wealthy and becomes richer by the day.

It is the obscene amounts of money at his disposal which makes him so dangerous. With every successful terrorist operation, following every televised "Israeli atrocity" committed against Palestinians, more and more people are willing to join and donate to his cause, including those living in the United States.

In fact, those living in the U.S., are a major source of funds. Indeed, the tentacles of bin Laden's tangled finances at one time even reached into the pockets of George W. Bush—the president of the United States.

Bin Laden has numerous supporters and maintains strong family ties with the members of numerous Arab communities in the United States—and this is well known to the FBI.

Those closely linked to bin Laden, own property, motels, and condominiums. He also has relations with businesses associated with satellite communications.

One of bin Laden's brothers has established a scholarship at Harvard. Another relative owns condominiums in Charlestown.

Yet other of his associates, such as Khalid bin Mahfouz, are involved in international finance and banking. Until he was arrested, Khalid bin Mahfouz had been a major source of funds that were going into the pockets of al-Qa'eda—bin Laden's hydra-head terrorist organization.

Tangled are the roots of terrorism.

The link is money: The Mighty Dollar.

According to the Federal Reserve, over 90% of all $100 bills, and approximately $250 billion in U.S. currency, are in the hands of foreigners.

The American dollar has become the accepted currency of choice in many parts of the world. And, the American dollar is what fuels and makes profitable the trafficking of drugs, arms, women, and terrorism.

So far reaching are these tentacles, so important is the dollar, that George W. Bush, when he was still a private businessman, may have unwittingly contributed to the growing financial empire of al-Qa'eda.

During the 1980s Bush was a partner with James Bath who had extensive contacts in the Middle East, and who also represented the business interests of Salem M. bin Laden, a half-brother of Osama.

Moreover, Bath was purportedly a CIA liaison to Saudi Arabia—during the same period when Bush Sr., was head of he CIA. Bath was apparently involved in illegally funneling Saudi money into the United States, and money from the United States to offshore banks—money that apparently found its way into the pockets of bin Laden.

It has also been alleged that Bath was in the aviation business, i.e. Skyway Aircraft Leasing Ltd., located in the Cayman Islands. According to court documents, Skyway Aircraft Leasing Ltd. was a front, and was actually owned by Khalid bin Mahfouz; the same Khalid bin Mahfouz, who was funneling money to al-Qa'eda.

Of course, during this time period, the 1980s, bin Laden was the good friend of the United States.

******

As is well known to the FBI, money freely flows from the U.S. to bin laden and to "charities" associated with al-Qa'eda. Bin Laden has numerous supporters, living in the U.S. who raise money for his cause.

However, what exactly the "cause" might be or what exactly the money might be used for, is often a mystery to those raising money or lending financial support.

But that doesn't stop them from wanting to donate. Many view bin Laden as a "freedom fighter" including those who immigrated from Arab countries to the U.S. because they wish to be free.

Unfortunately, it does not occur to many of his U.S. supporters that the "freedom" bin Laden is fighting, is their freedom. Our freedom. It is American that is under attack.

"Usually the local people aren't aware of the broader aims," says James Philips of the Heritage Foundation.

Many private individuals, that is, U.S. residents originally hailing from Islamic nations, donate to the "cause." and step forward to financially assist bin Laden or other terrorists groups, because they are sickened and outraged by what they perceive to be America's support for Israeli "terrorism" and atrocities against Palestinians.

"These people can seem like perfectly ordinary, law-abiding citizens until the call to 'jihad" — Holy war — comes," says Judith Miller, an expert in terrorism.

Many of these fund raising groups have been under investigation by the FBI.

U.S. officials have identified numerous groups and individuals, all residing in America, who have financial links to bin

Laden's terrorist network, al-Qa'eda. Often they raise funds, which are laundered in banks located in Europe and the Middle East, including Kuwait and Saudi Arabia.

However, according to government officials, it is impossible to make a move on these groups and their associates. Since they have entered the country legally and have not been involved in illegal activities since they arrived, they are untouchable. They are home free.

******

Yet another source of funding has come from none other than the United States government. Not only did many of the hijackers learn how to fly a plane in U.S. schools of aviation, but the U.S. government may have been providing some of the financing that made these ungodly attacks a nightmarish reality.

It has been known for over a decade that the drug trade provides a major source of funds for terrorists. In Afghanistan, drugs are big business. A large part of the economy is based on drug trafficking and the raising of opium-producing poppies. However, many of the dollars that flow into the country in exchange for drugs, are in turn used to buy weapons and to export terrorism.

Drugs and the opium trade are a major source of revenue for bin Laden. During the Clinton administration, the drug dealing-bin Laden link was well recognized and this was yet another reason being offered to justify punishing the Taliban rulers of Afghanistan.

Soon after taking power, however, President George W. Bush inexplicably ordered a change in U.S. policy toward the Afghanistan government. His administration immediately began making plans to provide financial aid to Afghan poppy farmers. Despite the fact that Afghanistan is a major source for heroin and opium and that the money from the drug trade was supporting terrorism, U.S. drug enforcement officials announced drug production was on the decline and that we should provide Afghanistan with millions of dollars to make up for the drug-money deficit.

On May 17, a $43-million grant to Afghanistan was announced by Secretary of State Colin L. Powell—an announcement that left international drug experts stunned.

Perhaps the Bush administration thought of the money as a bribe—a way to get the Taliban hooked and dependent on the American dollar. Perhaps they thought that the money was a way to buy off not just the Taliban but bin Laden.

Whatever the Bush administration was thinking, the signal was clear: The United States was not only willing to turn a blind eye to Osama bin Laden and Afghanistan's support for his terrorist activities, but America was willing to fund it.

Again, U.S. intelligence has known for years that the revenue from drug sales was a direct source of revenue for bin Laden and his organization. Several of the hijackers living in south Florida were in fact suspected by neighbors to be drug dealers.

Dealing in drugs provided bin Laden with millions of dollars in income that he could lavish on his terrorist operations. And, just as the flow of drug profits began to decline, threatening his ability to fund his illicit empire, the United States stepped in. Bin Laden now had a new source of income: the United States government, to the tune of $43 million dollars.

THEY WALK AMONG US

The United States is not so much a "melting pot" as it is a stew.

During the migrations of the 1800s and early 1900s, entire neighborhoods came to consist of a single ethnic group; Italians here, the Irish there. The next block over, the Jews.

Now days, it is not uncommon for ethnic communities consisting of tens of thousands of individuals all belonging to the same race or having the same ethnic identity, to congregate together, sometimes forming cities within cities.

More often, these large single-ethnic communities are spread out, with Arabs, Indians, Asians and so on, living on the same block and right next door.

In recent years, there has been a large migration of Arab peoples to the United States. They come in search of freedom.

Some states and some communities have large concentrations of Arab peoples. For example, over 20,000 Muslims have migrated from the Middle East to south Florida where they have taken up residence alongside the 10,000 Arabs that have for decades called America home.

Arabs have been welcomed to America and enjoy the same freedoms as all other Americans. Like Koreans, Vietnamese, Mexicans and the members of all other nationalities, Arabs have flocked here in search of the American Dream.

Yet others have been planted here in order to turn that dream into an American nightmare.

Some are spies. Some are potential saboteurs. Some raise money. And yet others recruit.

The FBI has known for years that bin Laden associates are firmly planted in the United States—like ticks burrowing in and sucking the life blood of the American people. At least five hard core groups of bin Laden sympathizers, are known to have been operating in the United States for the last five years.

Some work as university professors. Some in restaurants as cooks. Yet others as cab drivers.

Some work as cab drivers in the cities of Boston and New York. These cab drivers commonly ferry passengers to and from the World Trade Center, or to Boston's Logan Airport.

In fact, long before the September 11 attack, FBI agents knew that at least two Boston cab drivers, including Nabil Almarabh, were directly linked to Osama bin Laden.

Nabil Almarabh and another Boston cab driver, Raed Hijazi, were also linked to three of the hijackers and may have acted as a conduit for the flow of money that helped fund the attack.

Raed Hijazi shared more than a cab with at least two of the hijackers, he also shared an insane hatred for Americans. He is accused of plotting to kill American tourists in Jordan, on January 1, 2000.

Nabil Almarabh also harbored a fanatical hatred for Americans, wishing death upon those he would pass in the streets and who rode alone in his cab.

After the September 11 hijackings, when Nabil Almarabh's apartment was raided, FBI agents discovered three Arab men, drawings of airline flight plans and notations about an American military base.

According to the FBI, Nabil Almarabh, and possibly Raed Hijazi, frequently met with at least three of the hijackers, Al Suqami, Ahmed Alghamdi, and Hijazi, all of whom were also living in the Boston area,

In cities in Florida, Massachusetts, California, and other communities scattered throughout the United States, bin Laden agents would meet together at homes late at night, plotting, formulating plans, discussing how best to kill innocent American people.

Bin Laden terrorist cells have also been identified in Santa Clara, California—the heart of Silicon Valley, as well as Brooklyn, Tucson, Providence Rhode Island, Arlington Texas and South Florida.

One of the hijackers, Mohald Alshehri owned a luxurious condo at a private golf club in Hamletin Delray Beach, Florida. Over 30,000 Muslims make their home in south Florida, over 20,000 of whom are foreign born.

Terrorist cells have also been identified in Boston and in surrounding Massachusetts towns. At least three of the hijackers, Ahmed Alghamdi, Hijazi, and Saeed Alghamdi lived in Massachusetts and two of them had obtained Massachusetts driver's licenses; Ahmed Alghamdi in Cambridge, and Saeed Alghamdi in Salem. Ahmed Alghamdi had been living in Massachusetts since 1990.

According to U.S. officials it is standard procedure for the bin Laden organization to plant agents in a community with orders to blend in. This has been a bin Laden modus operandi for the last 10 years.

In preparing for the 1998 bombing of the U.S. Embassy in Kenya, bin Laden agents rented houses, married local women and lived in nearby communities for years prior to the attacks. These men also acted as spies. They gathered data and information on potential targets and helped to establish a local network that could help them commit their foul deeds.

The same pattern was implemented in the U.S.

Because bin Laden operatives have established their malignant cancerous roots in numerous American cities, candidates for terrorist training can be literally plucked from the streets and turned into walking time bombs, eager to do bin Laden's bidding and to achieve victory for Islam through martyrdom.

One of the terrorists, Saeed Alghamdi, who commandeered one of the Jets in the Kamikaze attack of September 11, had been in the United States since 1993.

Another of the hijackers, Waleed Alshehri resided in Daytona Beach, Florida, apprently on and off since 1994. He obtained a social security card that same year. Mr. Alshehri also had a pilot's license.

In 1999, however, he moved to Virginia. One can only surmise that he did not do this own a whim, but on orders from bin Laden.

Was he there to spy? Was he to recruit? Was he to organize? Or was he insane?

According to his father, Waleed Alshehri and his brother Wail, had traveled to the city of Medina in December 2000, to seek help for "psychological problems."

What we do know is that he made his neighbors nervous.

''There were always people coming and going,'' said Diane Albritton, a neighbor who lives across the street. ''Arabic people. Some of them never uttered a word; I don't know if they spoke English. But they looked very focused. We thought they might be dealing drugs.''

Hani Hanjour, one of the hijackers who commandeered the jetliner, which struck the Pentagon, had been living in Arizona since 1996. He in fact, appears to have been planted in the U.S. soon after the plot was launched. It was in 1996 that Mohamed Atta, the ostensible leader of the September 11, hijackings, wrote in his diary that he had decided to become a martyr.

In 1996, Hani Hanjour moved to the U.S. and paid for and received pilot training at CRM Airline Training Center in Scottsdale, Arizona. Six months before the attack, Hani Hanjour inquired about the possibility of receiving additional training on multi- engine planes. He was turned down, partly because of his attitude. He was perceived as a "difficult" person to train with.

Another hijacker, Salem al-Hamzi, lived in San Antonio, Texas.

Two other hijackers, Nawaq Alhamzi and Khalid Al-Midhar, apparently lived in San Diego for a number of years—San Diego having a large Muslim community. They rented a room in Lemon Grove, San Diego, from Abdussattar Shaikh, co-founder of San Diego's Islamic Center.

On September 11, Nawaq Alhamzi and Khalid Al-Midhar, joined Hani Hanjour in the hijacking of American Flight 77 which they crashed into the Pentagon.

Perhaps as many as half of the hijackers had lived among us for years.

They walked among us.

And the government of the United States knew it.

******

"I felt this jolt, like an earthquake, and then the building began to sway back and forth, back and forth.

I'm from California, and I don't like earthquakes, so the first thing that crossed my mind was to get out of the building.

Yet I hesitated. This was New York, not California. I was safe.

My phone rang.

It was my sister.

"There's a big hole in your building" she cried. "And there's smoke coming out of it."

I warned my coworkers and we ran out into the hall. There was a woman in a wheelchair. She was frightened and pressing the button for the elevator. Other people began crowding around her.

I ran to the stairwell. There was smoke and I could smell fumes, like kerosene.

There were people hurrying down from the upper floors. Some were burnt. Some were bloody. Some were talking on their cell phones as calm as can be.

By the time we reached the 40th floor, the entire stairwell was packed with people. I wanted to run, to get down as fast as I could, but I couldn't. We had to walk down single file.

Firemen were coming up, loaded down with gear. They looked so brave. So handsome. Firemen!

When we finally got to the lobby I was shocked. The elevators were blown out. The overhead sprinklers were on, and there was water and trash and shattered glass everywhere.

The elevators!

I thought about the woman in the wheelchair.

Every ten feet or so there was a rescue worker, giving directions, pointing us this way, then that way. Watch your step. Walk here. Don't stop there. I wanted to run, but I did what they told me.

I glanced at my watch. It had taken me almost an hour to get out.

I wanted to call my sister, but I had left my phone and hand-bag in my office. I didn't have any money and there was a long line in front of the pay phone.

I looked up then, and that's when I saw how bad it really was, both towers... and then I saw people... falling...

I couldn't stand it. I started walking, faster and faster. I had to get away.

Then I heard this terrible roar like some titanic unearthly beast.

People started running and screaming: "It's coming down. It's coming down. It's coming down."

I turned and looked back, and all I could see was a huge cloud of billowing gray smoke. It was rushing toward me. I could see people being swallowed up.

I kicked off my shoes and ran... but I wasn't fast enough. I curled up in a doorway, and was covered with dust.

Later, when I go up, I couldn't believe it. The towers... Everything was gone.

There was just this towering plume of smoke and dust—like it had been hit with an atomic bomb.

Then I remembered the faces of those firemen, heading up the stairs with all the gear on their backs. The look on those faces, those brave faces.

They must have known they were going to die.

I thought of their wives and children.

I couldn't stand it.

I started to cry.

— *A Survivor*

******

AFGHANISTAN, HAMBURG, HOMOSEXUALITY & TERRORISM:
TWISTED ARE THE ROOTS

Bin Laden is known to run terrorist training camps in eastern Afghanistan, with numerous base camps in the Nangarhar, Kunar, Paktia and Kandahar provinces.

Bin Laden knows he is a wanted man. A man with a price on his head.

He lives in the mountains to be closer to god.

There are hundreds of deep mountain caves in eastern Afghanistan, which offer seclusion and safety and privacy from prying eyes—including the eyes of American satellites and drones which periodically pass over head.

Some of these caves could even withstand an attack by an atomic bomb.

Bin Laden loves the mountains and the desert. His tribe is made up of desert people. Seclusion is not a luxury, it is a way of life that provides him time to study the scholars and to achieve a deeper understanding of the Koran and the mysteries of Allah, the great god.

Secluded, yes.

Isolated, no.

Although Bin Laden and his terrorists training camps are situated in the nearly inaccessible eastern mountains, he and his commanders and lieutenants are linked and can instantly communicate and send messages world-wide via high technology satellite dishes and satellite telephones.

Bin Laden is a modern scholar. His is no medieval mind. Technologically savvy, bin Laden is alleged to be the big money behind a major space telecommunications company that builds and launches communication satellites, which serve the entire

Middle East.

A terrorist with his own satellite is an extremely powerful enemy. He has the power to instantly communicate with his lieutenants wherever they are, world wide, and he may own the technology that would enable him to tap into and listen in to world wide communications, including those transmitted by the government of the United States.

The men that were specially chosen for martyrdom by the bin Laden organization, were also educated and technologically savvy. They were all well chosen and selected for their willingness to die for Islam.

These men, well-educated and disciplined, were willing to die in order to strike at the foes of Islam and rid their Muslim lands of American influence, to drive out the "American crusaders." Their weapon would be mass murder and mayhem.

Yet they too, were weapons, tools really, wielded by a master hand, who would conduct and orchestrate the mass murder of innocent women and men, from the eastern mountains of Afghanistan.

******

The terrorist Kamikaze suicide strikes on the financial and military centers of the United States were planned and carried out by many of the same "Afghan Arabs" who were implicated in the 1993 attack on the World Trade Center.

The men who carried out the dastardly deeds of September 11, had the same terrorist support networks and shared the same fanatical, twisted, religious and political ideology as Sheik Abdul Ahmed Rahman, who languishes in prison following the first attack on the World Trade Center.

These men, the Kamikaze terrorists, these merchants of mayhem, were linked directly to Osama bin Laden.

The attack on the Pentagon and the Twin Towers of the World Trade Center had bin Laden's fingerprints all over it. They were meticulously planned with military precision and carried out by individuals linked to his organization.

The attacks would be unprecedented in scope and sophistication.

The coordinated assault on America's political, military and financial capitals would wreck havoc and catch the United States government completely off guard — despite a massive law enforcement and intelligence network which exists solely to detect and thwart such attacks.

******

The plot to bring down the Twin Towers of the World Trade Center was hatched almost 10 years ago.

The first attempt, led by master terrorist, Ramzi Yousef, was carried out on February 26, 1993.

Ramzi Yousef didn't stick around to savor victory or to experience defeat. He instead returned to Afghanistan—the home base of bin Laden.

The first attack failed.

The terrorists would learn from their mistakes.

What they needed was more money and more explosive power.

Given enough money and explosive power they could transform Yousef's cataclysmic dream into a nightmarish reality.

They began to plan, and by 1996 the outlines of what would transform the skyline of Manhattan, into a nightmare moonscape of smoking rubble, began to take shape and form.

The plan would call for the training and deployment of four five-man teams who were to hijack and then pilot four commercial jetliners that would be transformed into fuel-laden guided missiles and then crashed into the Twin Towers of the World Trade Centers.

"It would be one of the most hideous crimes anyone had ever conceived."

Now came the next step: Recruiting and training the pilots

whose mission would be to fly and slam these planes into the Twin Towers, as well as the Pentagon and the White House—home of the President of the United States.

******

Suicide bombers from the Middle East are typically young, impressionable, often highly religious, and living in despair and hopeless poverty. They are loners. They are shy, awkward, and usually have few or no friends. In American slang, they are the "losers." They are young men with nothing to lose and everything to gain: Paradise and 70 willing virgins.

And like many virgins, these young men, these "losers," are often seduced by older men, who offer camaraderie and the chance to feel wanted, to belong and to have friends, if only the young man will agree to kill himself.

Friendless, awkward, shy and alone, these young men are easy pickings for those sophisticated in the art of enticing the friendless with gifts of kindness, respect and yes, even love, brotherly love.

The recruiters, these older men wise in the world, offer the "loser" a chance to become an accepted, respected member of the gang, part of an elite brotherhood: A brotherhood in blood.

Perhaps as many as half of the 19 men who agreed to kill themselves and thousands of others on September 11, were basically identical to the easily manipulated lost souls who volunteer for death in the Middle East.

Although Wail Alshehri was much older than the typical suicide bomber, he was approximately age 32, he suffered from significant "psychological problems" that required treatment.

Abdulaziz Alomari, age 21, was possibly an alcholic. He had at least one arrest for drunk driving.

Ahmed Salah Alghamdi, age 20, was highly religious and the graduate of a religious school—which is where he may have first been recruited. Ahmed suffered from the torment of sin. He knew himself to be a sinner. He was wracked by a pathological, almost delusional guilt, frequently asking others, such as his parents, to pray for him.

Al Haznawi, age 20, was also highly religious, as well as the son of a prayer leader at a mosque in the Saudi town of Baljurshi.

Highly religious, mentally disturbed, losers—the stereotype of the suicide bomber.

However, at least half of the 19 men who hijacked the four passenger jets in the September 11 attack on the USA, were well educated and technically savvy professionals. A few were even physical fitness buffs who regularly worked out at the local gym. And yet, many of these men were also "lost souls;" shy awkward losers in search of friendship and redemption for their sins—both real and imagined.

In American high school culture, the "loser" may also be a "nerd;" a technically savvy, intelligent young man, who nevertheless is so shy and lacking in social skills that he becomes isolated and alone.

Likewise, many of these intelligent young men, these terrorist Kamikazes, were "losers" and social misfits and some were drowning in self-hate.

Some would agree to murder and destroy Americans, only because they were seeking to destroy their own unknown face.

******

In the 12th century, the Catholic Pope, Urban II, recognized that in order to drive the Muslims from the Holy lands, he would need an army of men who would not recoil when asked to commit mass murder and the violist of atrocities in the name of God.

It was not the pious, or the religious, whom Urban called upon to go forth and make war, but murderers, rapists, molesters of children and even homosexuals.

"You oppressors of orphans, you robbers of widows, you homicides, you blasphemers, you plunderers of others' rights...

If you want to take counsel for your souls you must go forward boldly as knights of Christ..." so proclaimed the Pope who offered "indulgences" and redemption to all those who would commit blasphemies and murder women and children in the name of the Lord God and Jesus Christ.

Like Urban II, Osama bin Laden recognized that he would require an army of sinners if he was to win this war against the infidels. In 1996 he issued a call to arms that mirrors the call of Urban II, almost a thousand years before. Bin Laden welcomed sinners to his cause:

"The ultimate aim of pleasing Allah...and obeying His messenger... is to fight the enemy, in every aspects and in a complete manner... it is a duty to fight them even if the intention of the fighter is not pure i.e., fighting for the sake of leadership (personal gain) or if they do not observe the rules and commandments of Islam. It was the tradition of the people of the Sunnah (Ahlul-Sunnah) to join and invade- fight- with the righteous and non-righteous men.... It is not possible to fight except with the help of non-righteous military personnel and commanders [otherwise] those who are the greater danger to this life and religion, will take control...."

And, like Urban II, Osama bin laden offered a reward: Paradise, salvation and the forgiveness of sins.

Yet, unlike Urban II, Osama bin Laden also offered his army of sinners a world of material indulgences and delights. He provided them with cold hard cash. Lots of cash. Gobs of cash. Money, money, money.

Sinners, after all, need lots of spending money to support their sins and these men, his army of Kamikaze terrorists would have the chance to live it up before ending their sorry lives in an explosive terrifying airline crash. They would live it up because they did not have long to live.

******

Suicide bombers often know only that they will someday blow themselves up. They wait patiently for orders and the instructions are quite simple and provided usually on the day before the attack is to be carried out. Technical expertise and extensive training are not requirements. The bomber need only strap on an explosive backpack, wonder from their community into the land of their enemies, the Jews, and them blow themselves up.

By contrast, many of those who committed the September 11th atrocities, had lived in the United States for years and had basically blended in. They had also known the basics of what their mission entailed and had been receiving sophisticated and detailed training for years. Some of these men knew death was their fate from as far back as 1996.

Those who carry out suicide bombings in the Middle East are often under close supervision so that they are essentially under direct manipulative control of an older man—their "friend" and mentor.

The men who carried out the suicide attacks against America did so essentially by remote control well beyond the watchful eye of a supreme leader.

Even more remarkable is that they kept their plans secret for years.

"What happened on September 11 has demolished a number of our presumptions about suicide attacks," says Brian Jenkins, a terrorism specialist with the Rand Corporation. "It's possible to get one person to make that commitment and carry it out. But as you add a second, a third, a fourth, that chance increases on the way to the mission that somebody is going to say, 'This is a bad idea.' "

In this case, 19 men remained committed to a "bad idea," and they carried it out with sophistication and military precision.

MOHAMED ATTA

Mohamed Atta, 33, may not have been the supreme leader, but he was centrally involved in possibly all phases of the attack, including planning, spying, recruitment and training.

Atta was a religious man, which is a common characteristic of those who carry out suicide attacks. Yet, Atta differed from the stereotypical suicide attacker in that he was older, 33, highly educated and technically skilled. He also came from a well do family and could be considered "upwardly mobile."

In many respects he was no different from any other "upwardly mobile" highly educated Muslim. But there were also several notable exceptions. Atta drank alcohol excessively and he enjoyed hanging out at bars, including Sharky's Billiard Bar in Hamburg where he was attending the Technical University.

He also preferred the company of men to women and his goal in life was to launch a suicidal attack and murder thousands of people who had never caused him or his loved ones harm.

Mohamed Atta, was a religious man. His teachers described him as polite, diligent, intelligent and very religious, perhaps fanatically so.

Yet he was also a sinner who loved fast cars, flashy clothes, young men and money, lots and lots of money.

Mohamed Atta knew himself to be a sinner. He desperately sought redemption, turning first to religion, and then failing that, or perhaps, because of it, embracing suicide and mass murder in order to achieve martyrdom and to wash away his guilty sins.

Mohamed Atta was also a leader. He played a leadership role in Hamburg and again in the United States.

It is quite rare for an individual who plays such a central role in formulating a suicide mission, to actually take part in it; the exceptions being military engagements where soldiers and their leaders volunteer for a "suicide mission" and know they are facing certain death.

Atta considered himself to be a soldier. He knew he was

facing certain death and that his death would contribute to the death of thousands of innocent men and women. However, bin Laden had also offered him redemption and lots of cash.

"You oppressors of orphans, you robbers of widows, you homicides, you blasphemers, you plunderers of others' rights... If you want to take counsel for your souls you must go forward boldly..." and with the financial assistance of bin Laden's orgaization, they could go forwardly boldly with their pockets bulging with cash.

Thanks to the bin Laden orgazation, Atta could indulge his sinful life to the fullest and then wash away those sins in the blood of the innocents: by murdering innocent men and women who labored by day to earn their daily bread to support their loved ones and family.

Atta and his band of cutthroats didn't have to work. They bragged that they didn't have to work. They had a personal sugar daddy that showered them with cash—so much cash they couldn't spend it fast enough. On the day after their suicide attack on America, there was still over half a million dollars of spending money left in their bank accounts.

******

Mohamed Atta had signed up for the good life at least five years before he launched his Kamikaze attack.

In 1996 he made the decision: he would become a martyr.

He would also become a recruiter.

The money began pouring in.

It was a good investment.

Bin Laden had purchased a devil.

Young men were attracted to Mohamed Atta and many were seduced and convinced to join his army, including fellow hijackers, Marwan Al-Shehhi, Saeed Alghamdi and Ziad Jarrahi—men he met and "seduced" in Hamburg.

Together they were to do battle with the enemies of Islam and their reward would be paradise and the cleansing of their guilty sins.

Mohamed Atta saw himself as a soldier and he would lead his men on the journey to eternity and paradise.

However, his was not a suicide brigade preparing to do battle with a well-equipped enemy but with unarmed and unsuspecting civilians. He would maim and kill thousands of innocent people, murder husbands and wives who would never kiss their loved ones again. He would destroy whole families, make orphans of children, make widows and widowers of young women and men, and rip the hearts out of families who had never wished harm on the Arab peoples and who had never caused harm to him.

In the name of Islam, Mohamed Atta would dishonor Islam—which means peace. Mohammed Atta would live and die in sin.

****

ATTA & AL-SHEHHI

The plot began to take shape in Hamburg, Germany, in 1996. That same year Mohamed Atta wrote a letter in which he railed at Jews and Americans and then revealed that he planned to kill himself so he could go to heaven as a martyr.

Mohamed Atta had been given a mission. He was to help recruit and train several five-man suicide squads, which were to hijack American commercial jetliners and then crash them into the Twin Towers of the World Trade Center.

It was to be a six-year odyssey that would lead to the death of thousands of civilians. That odyssey would begin in Hamburg, a German city that is a well known safe haven for Islamic extremist groups and home to about 80,000 Muslims of various nationalities.

He was a man with a mission and his first goal was to recruit.

In 1996, Atta demanded that University officials accommodate his religious needs. He convinced them to establish an Islamic prayer room for himself and 20 other Muslim students.

Atta, the seductress, began recruiting others to the cause.

Arabic men not only attended his prayer room sermons but would gather late at night at his home.

According to the Kay Nehm, Germany's chief federal prosecutor, Atta organized a terrorist cell while in Hamburg, which included Islamic extremists directly associated with Osama bin Laden.

"These people were of Arabic background and lived in Hamburg and were Islamic fundamentalists. They formed a terrorist organization with the aim of launching spectacular attacks on the institutions of the United States."

Atta held meetings in the prayer room and in his home and soon found a willing convert, Marwan Al-Shehhi, who was 11 years his junior. Marwan Al-Shehhi, was not just a convert, he moved into Atta's apartment and formed an unusual relationship that was to last until the day they died.

The two men became "inseparable" and "joined at the hip."

They lived together. They trained together. They worked out together. They drank together. They committed mass murder together. The only thing they didn't do together was seek out women.

They had no interest in women.

In America and Europe, when two men form close, physical, "inseparable" relationships, and eschew the company of females, few eyebrows are raised even when it becomes clear the men are homosexuals.

In more conservative Islamic countries, it is also not uncommon for men to spend a lot of time together and to even live together. That two highly religious men might also become inseparable and eschew the company of women, would be viewed as a sign of virtue and no cause for alarm.

However, if the same two inseparable Arab men liked to

drink, wear expensive fancy clothes and spend time on the town, but also eschewed the company of women, such behavior would be recognized for what it is, and would not be tolerated. It would have been viewed as "immoral." Sinful.

Al-Shehh was also a problem drinker. In Florida he and Atta frequented a number of bars and were often observed to down four or five drinks in a row. Their favorite "poisons" included rum and Coke and Stolichnaya vodka and orange juice.

If they were Osama bin Laden's men, they didn't act like it. Bin Laden would not let his boys smoke cigarettes. Drinking alcohol would have led to banishment from the ranks of his al-Qa'eda movement.

However, as we now know, in 1996 bin Laden made an exception. He welcomed sinners into the ranks of his fighters. He would even finance their sins.

Were the two men homosexuals?

We don't know.

What we do know is that Mohamed Atta and Marwan Al-Shehhi were fashion conscious, they enjoyed wearing expensive clothes, and were provided with large sums of money to indulge these habits. They also spent time keeping their bodies pretty by working out together at gyms.

They were always together.

The lived together.

They were inseparable.

Indeed, these two men remained "bound at the hip" until the day they boarded separate planes in Boston and hijacked them to New York City.

That they were both highly religious, Mohamed Atta in particular, does not rule out homosexuality. It certainly didn't rule out mass murder. Rather their brand of religiosity leads credence to the possibility that these two fashion conscious, inseparable, unmarried men may have harbored "forbidden" tendencies, even if they never acted on them.

These forbidden tendencies may have also been the lure,

which attracted and then bound so many young men to Atta's camp. These same guilty, sinful tendencies may have had the motive force, which drove them to commit suicide and mass murder—devilish deeds that would cleanse them of their sins, even if they had never acted on them.

Mohamed Atta, at least while he was in Hamburg, Germany, had taken on the role of a cleric, of a priest!   In was in this clerical-type shepherd role that he was able to gather so many sheep.

Homosexuality is common among clerics, shamans and priests. In the United States, homosexuality was so rampant within the ministry of the Episcopal church and its homosexual clergy so openly promiscuous that the church lost over 5 million members by 1997.

According to Dr. Thomas Plante of the Jesuit college, Santa Clara University and the editor of a book on sexuality and the church, "50 percent of the Catholic clergy are gay, even though they're not acting on it."

In 1999, the Bishop of the Santa Rosa Diocese in California was forced to resign because another priest, a younger man, accused the Bishop of repeatedly raping him.

In 2000, the Catholic Chuch decreed that priests could no longer be alone with altar boys, because of the possibility these older men would seduce their young charges.

In Hamburg, Mohamed Atta also served a priestly role. He gathered young and highly intelligent Muslim men who were alone, friendless and isolated, and bound them to him and his cause. He was a seductress.

******

ZIAD JARRAH

Ziad Jarrah was seduced. He soon began living together with Mohamed Atta and Marwan Al-Shehhi in the same apartment—

111

an arrangement that astonished his father, Samir Jarrah, when he learned of it.

This unusual relationship also put a strain on Ziad's relationship with his fiance, Asle. Although they were to get married, Ziad became so entangled with his new friends that he no longer had time to see her. He was so busy that when it came time for Asle to meet his parents, he could not find the time to accompany her.

Too busy to bring his fiance to meet his family?

Ziad Jarrah was seduced. He not only lived with the two men but he died with them. On September 11, he helped to commandeer and then to pilot one of the four hijacked planes.

When Ziad Jarrah moved in with Mohamed Atta and Marwan Al-Shehhi, the Jarrah family realized that something was terribly wrong with their only son.

He was living with two men in a small apartment when he had more than enough money to live alone. His relationship with his fiance grew more and more estranged. He was behaving strangely. He was preoccupied. He seemed moody and depressed.

What was wrong with Ziad?

His family did not know.

What was troubling Ziad?

They did not know.

What we do know is that Ziad felt compelled to kill himself for Islam.

According to Islamic tradition and as instructed by "suicide teacher" Mohammed el Hattab, "He who gives his life for Islam will have his sins forgiven."

What sins had he committed? What had he done that was so utterly horrible that only a martyr's death could wash away his sins?

We do not know.

Yet, something so bothered the young man that he volunteered to participate in a mission of death that was guaranteed to end his painful life and cleanse him of his guilty sins.

But first, he had to make a pilgrimage.

His fiance called his family to report that Ziad disappeared from Hamburg. He had been gone for five weeks.

Later it was discovered that he had traveled to Afghanistan— the home base of bin Laden.

At the end of that five weeks, Ziad Jarrah set off for the United States.

Of the 19 men who participated in the Kamikaze hijacking of the four American jetliners, Ziad Jarra most closely resembled the profile of the suicide bomber.

He was reserved and shy and when he was 7 years old, he had been traumatized by Israeli soldiers. In 1982, during the Israeli siege of Beirut, the Jews had invaded his village with their high powered American-made weapons, and began killing people.

The Jews were always killing Arab people. Now Mohamed Atta and his patron, Osama bin Laden, gave him an opportunity to strike back at the hated Jews, their American ally and destroy his own unknown face.

******

"Steal girders groaned and giant slabs of broken concrete threatened to topple on top of us at any moment. Everywhere, body parts, a leg, an arm, bodies that had been so badly burned it was impossible to tell if they were human.

"And still, there seemed to be people alive, buried beneath the rubble, broken and trapped and unable to get away from the searing heat and the fires."

"People were screaming. The air was hot and thick with dust...slivers of glass were still falling like daggers from the sky... twisted steel girders lay strewn among the ground, chunks of concrete lay helter-skelter among the ruins. Fires burned all around us...and victims, trapped beneath the rubble, were dialing 911 on their cell phones, desperately clinging to life and crying, begging for help."

—A Rescue Worker

"We tried to get to them but we were helpless... there was simply no way anyone could fight through the searing heat to reach those calling for help. The hellish heat... the fires... everything was red hot... it must have been over 2,000 degrees. There was nothing we could do. They were screaming, crying... but there was nothing we could do."

—A Rescue Worker

******

FLYING HIGH IN FLORIDA

Mohamed Atta, Marwan Al-Shehhi, Ziad Jarrahi, Hani Hanjour, Abdul Alomari, Saeed Alghamdi, Khalid Al-Midhar, Waleed M. Alshehri, and 11 other hijackers belonged to an elite group of "Islamic soldiers." They would become martyrs and would kill themselves and thousands of innocent people for what they believed was a just cause — one founded on hate and a perversion of Islamic principles. These men would occupy leading roles in commandeering and piloting the four planes, which were to strike at the heart of America.

Mohamed Atta was clearly the leader, in Hamburg and again in the United States. Atta was now preparing to implement the final phase of the deadliest attack ever experienced by the American people.

On September 11, 2001, Mohamed Atta would forcefully take the controls of American Airlines Flight 11, Al-Shehhi would pilot United Airlines Flight 175, Hani Hanjour and his men would hijack American Airlines Flight 77 and Ziad Jarrahi and his band of cutthroats would seize United Airlines Flight 93. Two of the jets would strike and destroy the twin towers of the World Trade Center. The third jetliner, would strike the Pentagon, the symbol of America's military might. The team headed by Ziad Jarrahi had a different target: The White House, the home of the President of the United States.

******

In July 2000, Marwan Al-Shehhi and Atta, who carried a Saudi passport, traveled from Germany to Florida. They told people they were "cousins."

Like so many other foreign nationals from China, Korea,

South America, Europe and the Middle East, Atta and his "cousin" enrolled in Huffman Aviation International flight school in Venice, Florida, to receive flight training. They said they wanted to be pilots and were hoping to fly corporate jets in the United Arab Emirates.

They had a lot of money. They liked to flash their cash.

Both men paid $10,000 for four months of pilot training on small planes.

Atta and Marwin also polished their aviation skills at another flight school, the SimCenter Inc., near Miami. They paid $1,500 each for a three-hour course. They trained on a flight simulator for a Boeing 727 jet.

A flight simulator provides a student with a realistic flying experience over realistic terrain, including mountains, rivers, forests and the World Trade Center. In fact, the World Trade Center is featured in software flight simulator packages. Their function is to familiarize pilots who intend to fly planes over New York.

Atta and his "cousin" intended to crash their planes into New York—and this experience too can be obtained from a flight simulator.

Once the door to the room housing the flight simulator is closed, whatever students do behind those closed doors, including practice runs at slamming into the Twin Towers of the World Trade Center, would be known only to themselves. They obtained three hours of practice.

Henry George, an instructor, said Atta "got a good feel for maneuvering the airplane around, basically turning the airplane left and right, climbing and descending."

Atta was slowly acquiring the skills to maneuver a Boeing 727 into the heart of the Twin Towers of the World Trade Center.

******

Rudy Dekkers, President and owner of Huffman Aviation, reported that Atta and Marwin Al-Shehhi began attending flight school in July 2000. Huffman offers training in light, single-engine aircraft not commercial jetliners.

Atta and Marwin attended Huffman Aviation for about five months and never completed there training. The men explained by saying they were leaving in order to take advanced instruction elsewhere.

In the few remaining weeks before the September 11 terrorist attack, the two "cousins" paid $88.00 an hour for advanced training at another school. They rented a single engine plane, in order "to increase their flying hours" and to hone their skills. However, they were not interested in receiving advanced training in takeoffs and landings—theirs was to be a crash landing directly into the heart of America.

"He said he was already a pilot and was not after another license," reported Andrew Law, a flight instructor. "He said he was just practicing, showing his friend the airplane and what to expect."

What they expected, was to become martyrs. What they wanted, was to kill thousands of people.

******

A former employee at Huffman Aviation, Charlie Voss and his wife Drew welcomed the two foreign nationals, and allowed them to stay in their home while attending flight school at Huffman. They told Charlie and Drew they had just arrived in the U.S. from Hamburg, Germany.

"We are cousins," they said.

They were also rude and unpleasant and rewarded the generosity of Drew and Charlie Voss by leaving messes in their wake that they expected Drew to clean up. The two cousins were decidedly unfriendly.

After a week of what Voss described as arrogant, condescending, inconsiderate behavior, Drew Voss decided she had had enough. "They were rude, selfish, unfriendly and I kicked them out!"

Atta and Marwin Alshehhi moved out and set up house-keeping in an apartment they rented in Coral Springs, which is near Fort Lauderdale, Florida. Although their neighbors tried to make them feel welcome the two "cousins" were not very friendly and did not socialize; that is, with Americans.

The two men made it clear they did not particularly care for Americans.

While attending the flight school, they refused to socialize with the others and kept a very low, but angry, profile.

"They seemed different, moody," said Richard Nyren, a student at the school. "You would never see them smile."

Another student, Azzan Ali, recalled that they often ranted about Israel, were "very religious... and they liked to brag about their wealth."

They were special. They were adverse to work or holding down a job. And why should they? They had a sugar daddy and a license to sin.

"We don't want to work," they told Nyren.

As summed up by one of the flight instructors: "They didn't talk to anyone about anything at all. They were not very friendly. They made it clear they were not interested in making friends. If you tried to strike up a conversation they would stare at you, as if you were some kind of insect. They often seemed angry and preoccupied, like they had a lot on their minds."

What they had in mind was mass murder.

As related by Mark Mikarts, a Huffman flight instructor: "Atta was not a friendly person. He got into conflicts with a lot of guys here, including myself and another flight instructor."

"Atta and I got into an altercation once because I warned him that what he was doing was dangerous. During our training flights he kept jerking the yoke back and pulling the nose of the plane up to a very dangerous angle, to the point where it would stall."

"Even though I reprimanded him for putting us in a danger-ous situation, he did it again and again. After I reprimanded him yet again, he got upset and demanded that the flight school give him another instructor. But within days he was having altercations with that instructor too."

Atta had a bad temper. On the night before the September 11th attack, he got into an altercation with another driver at Logan International Airport.

Atta and Marwin Alshehhi didn't just dislike Americans; they hated them. Atta and Alshehhi were drowning in hate, perhaps even self-hate and sometimes they drowned their hate in alcohol.

When not training, or hanging out together in the privacy of their room, the two "joined at the hip" cousins liked to dress up in fancy expensive clothes, take a ride in Atta's flaming red Pontiac, and hit the bars. But not the trendy "pick up" bars, rather the kind of bars where men congregate together and seek solace in drink.

Yet, they were also not adverse to going to bars where ladies might be present—especially if the bar offered the two men the opportunity to humiliate the hated opposite sex, i.e. strip clubs: establishments where they sometimes met with their coconspirators. They would drink together, get drunk, humiliate the ladies and brag that they were pilots.

A nude dancer at the Cheeta remembered that Atta liked to throw $100 bills on the floor, and then order the girls to crawl on their knees to pick them up.

In the days after the hijacking, Gus Renny, owner of the Palm Beach bar, immediately recognized him and his drinking buddy when shown photos by the FBI.

"I told the FBI that those two guys were in here last week bragging they were Arab pilots-and they spent over a $1000 in 45 minutes," said Gus. "They ordered several rounds of drinks and then some of our most expensive champagne-a bottle of Krug and a bottle of Perrier-Jouet."

In the weeks before the attack, the two men met a third man at Shuckums, a sports bar in Hollywood, Florida. When the FBI showed manager Tony Amos photos and mug shots, he immediately recognized the two "cousins."

Even though it was midday and the religion of Islam forbids alcohol, Atta was knocking down vodka while Marwan drank rum and Coke. There was a third man, possibly Ziad Samir Jarrahi, or more likely, Abdul Alomair, who was also drinking heavily.

As they knocked down drink after drink, Marwan and the third man began arguing—lovers quarrel perhaps?

"There were a lot of hand gestures and Al-Shehhi was definitely upset," Amos said.

Atta had no interest in the quarrel and instead occupied himself by playing Trivial Pursuit and blackjack.

"He looked nervous," manager Tony Amos said. "He kept putting dollars in and he was really focused."

The men continued to drink. It was daylight and they were getting drunk.

"They each had five drinks. They were becoming more and more intoxicated and growing louder and louder. One of them, his voice was so slurred and he had such a thick accent, it was difficult to understand what he was raving about. The only thing I remember is that he said he was a pilot."

They were nasty drunks. Loud and belligerent, even arguing with the bartender over the bill.

Mohamed snarled at the bartender and announced in a loud drunken voice that he "worked for American Airlines and made a lot of money."

When Tony Amos, the manager, came over to see what was wrong, Atta produced a wad of $100 bills and paid. But not before cursing Amos: "You think I can't pay my bill? I'm a pilot for American Airlines. I can pay my fucking bill."

The two drunks and their friend finally paid their $48 tab and drove away in Atta's 1989 flaming red Pontiac.

Days after the attack, FBI agents located a 1989 red Pontiac that had been abandoned at Boston's Logan Airport. It was registered to Mohamed Atta.

FLORIDA: HIJACKER HEAVEN

Florida was hijacker heaven. An incredible number of hijackers and their associates flocked to Florida and set up residence in a number of south Florida cities and towns—under the supposed watchful eyes of the FBI.

Eighteen men on the FBI's watch list suspected of being potential terrorist threats to the United States lived in the general vicinity of Vero Beach. Eight of these men and two of the hijackers, Hamza Alghamdi and Ahmed Alghamdi, shared a dormitory at Flight Safety International, a flight school in Vero Beach.

In fact, 14 of the 19 hijackers called Florida their home sweet home.

Two of the hijackers, Waleed Alshehri and Saeed Alghamdi, and yet another man suspected of being a terrorist threat, shared an address in Daytona Beach. Waleed Alshehri and his brother Wail also shared yet another address with a woman living in Hollywood, Florida. The woman, Ms. Alshehri, was also on the "watch list."

Waleed and Wail Alshehri would be part of the team, captained by Atta, which would commandeer Flight 11 and then smash it into the World Trade Center.

Yet, another hijacker, Abdul Alomari, rented a $1400-a-month pastel stucco house next door to another Saudi, in Hollywood Florida. He lived there with his veiled wife and four children

Like Atta and Marwan Al-Shehhi, Alomari was a drunk. He was a reckless drunk and had an arrest record for drunken driving.

Atta, Al-Shehhi and Alomari loved to drink, were fancy dressers, they spent a lot of cash and they enjoyed the fast life. They spent a lot of time in strip clubs, throwing money at the strippers as they drank and partied.

Yet, not all of the hijackers were single men nursing forbidden impulses or drinking to the point of drunkenness.

Mohald Alshehri was a family man who owned a luxurious condo at the private golf club Hamlet in Delray Beach, Florida. There he lived with his veiled wife and children.

His neighbors tried to make the Alshehri family feel welcome.

His children played with his neighbor's children. They were invited to slumber parties and played Nintendo together. As his children were attending classes at a local school, he was in school as well, flight training school, at Flight Safety Academy. Although his wife was heavily robed and seldom allowed out of the house, outwardly Mohald Alshehri and his wife lived the lives of an Arabic Ozzie and Harriet.

"The only problem," reported neighbor Betty Egger, "were the late-night meetings. Sometimes as many as a dozen cars would be parked outside," some on her own lawn.

Another of the terrorists, Ahmed A. al-Ghamdi lived in Pensacola. His apartment was the center of considerable activity, especially late at night. Large numbers of Arab men typically arrived after dark for prolonged meetings.

According to Linda Green, a neighbor, ''People would come and knock on the doors late at night. We might see three or four of them arriving together, and they were always men. It was always in the evening. The traffic in and out, was constant every evening. They would go and knock, and then it would be a little while and someone would look out the window to see who it was, like they were being very cautious. Not your normal coming to the door and opening it.''

Three of the hijackers maintained a residence next door to sisters, Nicole and Rachel Diaz, in Del Ray Beach.

"I never once saw one of them smile. You'd get in the elevator and they wouldn't even acknowledge that you were in there with them," 12-year-old Nicole said.

"They would always be carrying medium-size bags with

them," added Rachel, 14. "I never saw them without those bags. A lot of people here said they must be drug smugglers."

Two other hijackers, Ahmed Alnami and Saeed Alghamdi, lived in a two-bedroom apartment numbered 1504, at the Delray Racquet Club.

Like most of the other hijackers, Ahmed Alnami and Saeed Alghamdi, did not care for Americans. They were rude, arrogant and "extraordinarily unfriendly."

"I rode the elevator with them 20 times and never ever did they say hi, even though I always did," said Stacy Warm, a neighbor.

A lot of Arab men would also congregate at their apartment in the evening—including men on the FBI's "watch list."

"There were at least four of them but my husband said he counted as many as seven. Sometimes an older guy would be seen with them." Often these men would visit late at night.

They didn't like Americans. They were going to kill Americans. Thousands of Americans.

"They wouldn't look at you in the eye. It was like you didn't even exist. They always had duffel bags or gym bags with them, wherever they went, even to the pool. I thought they were drug dealers," she said.

Maybe they were.

******

Drugs are an important source of revenue for terrorists and for the economies of the nations that harbor them.

So important that when poppy and thus opium production declined in Afghanistan—home of bin Laden—Colin Powell and the Bush administration stepped forward and provided a $43 million grant to the Taliban government.

The hijackers were also flush with cash. They had expensive tastes. They were living it up and flashing lots of cash.

These men traveled widely throughout Florida, frequently met together in a variety of locations, drank together, worked out together and plotted mass murder together. They left their "fingerprints" everywhere: airports, motels and especially bars. And always, like always, they flashed lots of cash, wads and wads of $100 bills.

Gus Renny, owner of the Palm Beach bar, said Atta and another man "spent more than $1000 in 45 minutes."

They were fancy dressers, they spent a lot of cash, and they liked the fast life, spending a lot of time not only in bars, but strip clubs.

One of their favorite watering holes was the 44th Aero Squadron, a bar located at the Venice airport in Florida. "Atta was a very big spender. He also carried a wad of $100 bills," said Keith Schortzmann, the bar's owner, "enough to choke a horse."

They were living it up, because they did not have much longer to live.

******

One of the few and notable exceptions to the mass concentration of hijackers in Florida may have been Ziad Jarrahi. The FBI turned up evidence that he had been living a somewhat Spartan existence in an $800-a-month apartment in Brooklyn.

Yet other evidence suggests that Ziad also moved to Florida and frequently met with Atta and the other terrorists.

Why Florida?

The hijackers may have chosen Florida for a number of reasons, including the warm weather and perhaps the chance to ogle decadent Western females as they pranced nearly naked in string bikinis on south Florida's famed white sand beaches.

All that sand, it may have reminded them of their own desert kingdoms.

They may have also believed they were less likely to stand out and draw attention in Florida, as compared, for example, to Vermont or South Dakota. Over 30,000 Muslims live in South Florida, the vast majority of whom are foreign-born. In fact, several of the hijackers had been living in Florida for years, including Mohald Alshehri who owned a luxurious condo at a private golf club in Delray Beach.

The dark-skinned Arabs may have also felt they would be less conspicuous because Florida is also the home of millions of dark skinned Latin peoples.

Also, Florida attracts a flood of tourists year round, over 70 million in 2000. The fact that these men were jobless and without any obvious means of supporting themselves financially, but were nevertheless spending gobs of cash, would have gone virtually unnoticed. They would have easily blended in with the millions of other rich foreigners who come to the U.S. every year to stay, play and have fun.

These men, however, were here to commit mass murder. They had come to Florida to train. The hijackers would obtain the training they needed to kill thousands of Americans, in the friendly Florida skies of the USA.

******

It was precisely because their mission was murder that these men and their supporters and back up crews chose Florida. Florida has a unique status second only to California, and it has nothing to do with Florida oranges.

Florida has an incredible concentration of flight schools offering aviation instruction. Florida boasts more than 225 flying schools, including those sponsored or offered at Florida's public airports.

Because Florida is number 2, they "try harder" and anyone who wants to learn how to fly a jet in order to commit mass murder can easily obtain the requisite training—no questions asked; other than: Show me the money. In Florida, training in aviation is a $1-billion-a-year industry.

And, as many as 30 percent of the students are foreigners Florida was the perfect location.

The terrorists could travel freely, could obtain the training they desired and could frequently meet together to plot the murder of thousands of innocent people and the destruction of the fabled Twin Towers.

As long as they paid in cash, there were no questions asked, even when they declined instruction in landing and takeoffs.

That they were Arabs speaking with halting foreign accents and hated Americans and made no secret of their dislike, was not all that unusual.

"It's unlikely that these men would have stood out just because they come from another country," said Gary Kitely, executive director of the University Aviation Association. "Students from all over the world come to this country to learn how to fly."

******

Many of the hijackers were already pilots and need minimal training, although how many is unclear. For example, Abdulaziz Alomari told neighbors that he was a pilot and claimed to work for a subcontractor of Saudi Arabian Airlines.

Alomari listed his address as Jeddah, Saudi Arabia, according to FAA records. He also listed his previous employer as Saudi Flight Ops, which handles maintenance for Saudi Arabian Airlines at Kennedy airport in New York.

Many of the hijackers and their associates received flight training at Flight Safety International, which is under contact with Saudi Arabian Airlines, the kingdom's national airline.

Some of these men received funding from the Saudi government, which paid for their training. Al Shehri, for example, received a four-year scholarship for flight training at the school, money granted by the Saudi Arabian government.

There is also evidence to suggest that some of the hijackers had piloted jets for the Saudi Arabian military.

However, it has been suggested that some of the hijackers had stolen the identities of pilots employed in Saudi Arabia and that most of the hijackers were not really Saudi citizens or pilots. Why they would bother to perpetrate such a hoax is unclear particularly in that many of these men were in fact pilots and knew how to fly a plane.

Of course, if the identities given by the majority of these men are real, this would suggest that the hijackers were recruited from the cream of Saudi society, including, perhaps from the Saudi military and the Saudi government, by Osama bin Laden, or some other terrorist group. In fact, it has been alleged and vehemently denied, that Alshehri, was the son of a Saudi Arabian diplomat. Alshehri also claimed to have been a pilot working for the Saudi Arabian airlines, which is government owned and operated.

There has since been some grumbling from congressional leaders when they found out that many of the hijackers received assistance in entering the U.S. from Saudi military and government personnel.

"The Saudi government has some serious explaining to do," commented one administration official.

Why would the sons of Saudi diplomats and government officials and members of the Saudi government and military assist in a terrorist attack on America?

"It is not possible to fight except with the help of non righteous military personnel and commanders."

— Osama bin Laden

Bin Laden's tribe also hails from Saudi Arabia and almost half the hijackers come from families that have lived in the same area for hundreds of years.

The U.S military has established a base in Saudia Arabia, the holiest of the holy lands.

According to Islamic tradition: There shall be never again be two religions in Arabia.

The U.S. presence was an afront to God. Now the U.S. would suffer the wrath of god —perhaps with the help of "non righteous military personnel and commanders" working and living in Saudi Arabia.

******

Although several of the hijackers, and dozens of their associates were on the FBIs "watch list," these merchants of mayhem frequently met together not only in private but in public. They frequently drew attention to themselves. In their late night meetings, so many men would gather that they would park on neighbor's lawns.

Atta may have been present at many of those meetings.

Atta and Alshehhi would frequently take a drive in Atta's red 1989 Pontiac and visit with four of their fellow hijackers who were living in Delray Beach: Fayez Ahmed, Ahmed Alghamdi, Hamza Alghamdi, and Mohald Alshehri belonged to the terrorist cell that would be captained by Marwan Al-Shehhi.

They likely rehearsed their plans.

Fayez Ahmed, Ahmed Alghamdi, Hamza Alghamdi and Mohald Alshehri were to brandish knives and "bombs," to frighten the crew and then kill the pilots. The pilots had to be killed, because the hijackers knew that even if they held a gun to the man's head, he would not crash his jet into the Pentagon, White House, or the World Trade Center.

They likely practiced tying up the pilots, and then stabbing them to death.

Once the pilots were dead, Marwan Al-Shehhi would pilot United Airlines Flight 175 and crash it into the south Tower of the World Trade Center.

Atta would take out the north Tower.

Hani Hanjour and his team would attack the Pentagon.

Atta, appears to have also held clandestine meeting with Saeed Alghamdi, Ahmed Alhaznawi and Ahmed Alnami. These men comprised the core membership of the terrorist battle group that were captained by Ziad Jarrahi. Their mission: United Airlines Flight 93 would be hijacked after leaving the International Airport in Washington D.C., and would be slammed into the White House—home of the President of the United States.

FINAL PLANS: THE DIVINE WIND

The World Trade Center, a symbol of America's technological and economic world dominance, had been a terrorist target since 1993.

The 1993 plot to topple the World Trade Center failed because of insufficient explosive power.

The terrorists had learned from their mistakes.

If they were to be successful in their next attempt at terror, they would need a weapon with sufficient firepower to bring down the Twin Towers of the World Trade Center. Although possessing incredible explosive and killing potential, a missile was still insufficient.

The problem was studied by the best minds in the bin Laden organization. They examined their past failures and triumphs, in order to conjure up a new operational plan.

The bin Laden organization does not act on impulse or whim. They formulate their tactics by watching how their adversaries react to feints and threats. They probe for gaps and weaknesses to take advantage of any Achilles' heels they discover, to exploit them for future missions of mass destruction.

These terrorists also know they are being watched and sometimes they make it easy for the CIA and other intelligence organizations to observe their movements. Yet the terrorists know they are being watched and all the while are observing and learning from those who are unknowingly being analyzed by the very organization they are watching.

The spies are often spied upon.

Bin Laden has eyes and ears that even hover above the globe.

Terrorist organizations will sometimes "leak" their plans in order to listen and observe how America reacts and the steps she takes to defend the people and the nation. In this way terrorists acquire the information necessary to avoid our defenses. They also learn what steps were not taken so these security gaps may be exploited in a future operation.

The new plan, probably first conceived in 1996, required a "missile" with sufficient explosive power that it could bring down the Twin Towers and kill thousands of the polytheist infidels—the children, parents, and husbands and wives of the "American Crusaders."

How could they acquire such a "missile" and then fire it close to American shores?

The terrorists hit upon a plan.

The perfect weapon would be a massive, fuel-laden jet, a Boeing 767. The fuel tank of a Boeing holds 20,450 gallons of jet fuel. Although jet fuel is not as volatile as gasoline, it packs a powerful punch. A single gallon can produce 125,000 BTUs of energy. A Boeing 767, weighing 351,000 pounds and fully loaded with jet fuel, would have the explosive power of a one-kiloton nuclear bomb!

The hijacking of airlines had become commonplace during the 1970s and 1980s and then faded in popularity. Every terrorist organization worth its salt knows that airplanes, especially those departing from American soil, are easy targets. American pilots are even trained to cooperate with hijackers in order not to risk human lives.

Yet, it was also known, or at least well publicized that airline security had been "beefed up." The bin Laden organization needed to know how difficult it would be to place armed agents on a commercial jetliner.

Bin Laden's organization began testing commercial airline security in the United States. They targeted a number of airports, including Los Angeles International.

In one well-known incident, Ahmed Ressam, an Algerian citizen living in Montreal, Canada, placed a dummy suitcase near a ticket counter and another near a crowded area. His mission: to determine how long it took for airline security or one of the thousands of passengers passing through the terminal to become suspicious.

After studying and probing for weaknesses in the domestic airline industry for at least 8 years, bin Laden's people decided that they had learned enough.

And what they learned was that one of our greatest weaknesses was the U.S. commercial airline industry. They learned how easy it would be to smuggle in weapons and take control of a fully loaded jetliner. They also learned how to fly them precisely into American landmarks.

But not just any American Landmark: The Twin Towers of the World Trade Center. Secondary targets would include the Pentagon and the White House.

The airlines themselves had demonstrated how ridiculously easy it is to smuggle in knives, guns, pipe bombs and rope to tie up uncooperative pilots. In some studies, over 90 percent of individuals armed with weapons passed unchallenged through security checkpoints. In test after test it was discovered that plain clothes security were able to walk right passed airline security agents with packages, suitcases and backpacks—all of which could easily conceal weapons and bombs.

A particularly effective means of gaining entry without being detained or checked, was to follow an airline employee, or a janitor as they strolled around security checkpoints. And if the individual himself was carrying a bucket or a mop, he was almost never challenged.

U.S. airports are usually guarded by poorly trained, poorly paid, and poorly motivated security guards. Even when easily identified, lethal weapons often pass through baggage X-ray machines without being challenged.

The terrorists realized that airline security in the U.S. was little more than a hoax.

As summed up by David Stempler, President of the Air Travelers Association, a Washington-based lobbying organization for airline passengers, "We created a facade of security. The reality is that we did not perceive that we had much of a risk in this country. We had a system that was set up for failure."

The procedures were designed to meet government regulations and to assure the public it was safe to fly. The procedures were a sham. Everyone knew it was a sham.

This complacency would have fatal consequences.

The terrorists knew that airport security was not an obstacle that would hamper their mission.

They would smuggle weapons on board with the greatest of ease, and then use threats, a few box cutter knives and the element of surprise to accomplish their deadly deeds. Their weapon: Long-range passenger jetliners heavily laden with fuel, commercial jets that could be diverted to fly directly into the Pentagon and the World Trade Center, the symbols of American financial power and military might.

The plan, however, required that the jets selected for the hijackings would have to be fully fueled.

The hijackers would commandeer Boeing jets that were scheduled for cross-country flights.

Employing a fuel consumption calculator the terrorists made the necessary calculations: A fully fueled Boeing holds 20,450 gallons of jet fuel. During a cross-country trip it could burn up to 4,000 gallons an hour or more.

Conclusion: In order to obtain the most massive explosive effect and the greatest killing power, the jets must be hijacked soon after take off. It would be necessary to depart from airports located close to their targets.

The number one target was the World Trade Center.

The terrorists had several airports to choose from.

They began to probe and test security. They also did their homework.

The solution: Boston's Logan Airport.

Logan was notorious for its inattentiveness to security. During a single two-year period ending in 1999, there had been over 136 violations. Security was so poor that the port authority and the major airlines at Logan were fined a total of $178,000 for lapses in security.

Globe Aviation Services Corp. of Irving, Texas, and Huntleigh USA Corp. of St. Louis were responsible for operating the security checkpoints for the two targeted airlines at Logan. During tests, security checkpoints routinely failed to detect the presence of weapons and other smuggled contraband.

In 1999, a teen-age boy was able to circumvent the checkpoints altogether. He strolled across the tarmac, settled into an empty seat on a British Airways jet and flew to London.

Boston's Logan Airport was the ideal target. Logan was located close to the New York area and planes were constantly departing from the airport. Coupled with lax security, Logan was an obvious choice.

The terrorists would hijack not just one, but two wide bodied fuel-loaded commercial airplanes departing from Logan. Two more would be hijacked after takeoff from the International Airport near Washington, and the airport in Newark, New Jersey.

The Boeings were the perfect bomb, well suited for a Kamikaze-type attack on the Pentagon and New York's World Trade Center.

******

Atta and several of his men first began casing Logan International Airport in the year 2000, almost 12 months before launching their Kamikaze hijacking. They took a number of test flights and became increasingly familiar with airport security.

Likewise, the hijackers cased Ronald Reagan International Airport and the airports in New Jersey and Portland, Maine.

In the weeks before the September 11 hijackings, Hani Hanjour, the suspected pilot of American Airlines Flight 77, set up a base of operations outside Washington, in suburban Maryland. He and his four man hijacking team rented rooms at two motels on Route 1 in Laurel.

Not satisfied with his experience at the controls of a flight simulator, Hani Hanjour, the suspected pilot of Flight 77, paid an instructor at Freeway Airport in Bowie to guide him on three flights over Washington in August.

Hani Hanjour and his four-man team also cased the airport on at least five different occasions. It is likely that they also took several test flights.

The terrorists had also given considerable thought to the perfect day for a hijacking. They checked and rechecked flight schedules to determine the optimal day for a hijacking.

Typically, most people traveling cross-country do not chose Tuesdays to take their flights. Often these jets are less than half full.

Perfect!

A commercial jet with just a few passengers would be easier to hijack with just a few men armed with knives and a fake bomb.

The choice was clear.

The hijackings would take place on a Tuesday.

September 11, 2001 fell on a Tuesday.

******

The terrorists began purchasing tickets in late August.

On August 28, Mohamed Atta purchased his final ticket for his final flight. Using a Visa credit card, Atta bought a ticket for a connecting flight from Portland, Maine, to Boston and a second ticket for a seat on American Airlines Flight 11.

They had gone through a dress rehearsal, perhaps many of them, and were now ready for the final act.

Atta, being fond of the Internet, bought his ticket from the American Airlines Web site and used a frequent-flier number that he had established three days before. His was seat 8D.

Another member of the Flight 11 hijacking team, paid cash for his ticket, and was to sit in 10B.

Waleed al-Shehri and his brother, Wail purchased seats 2B and 2A.

Nothing but the best for those who were to hijack United Airlines Flight 175. Using the Internet, two of the men paid United Airlines nearly $2000 each for one-way first-class seats, both of which were located close to the cockpit. Ghamdi paid $1760 for business-class Seat 9D. Hamza al-Ghamdi paid $1600 for his seat, 9C. Both men were trained pilots and would be sitting close to the cockpit.

The target for American Airlines Flight 77 was the Pentagon. Again, the Internet was the choice method for purchasing tickets. Nawaf al-Hamzi booked his ticket through the Internet travel agency, Travelocity.

Khalid al-Mihdhar, also used the Internet and booked his reservation on the American Airlines Web site. However, Khalid al-Mihdhar did not use a credit card but drove to the Baltimore-Washington International Airport on September 5 and paid for his ticket with cash. His seat was 12B.

Majed Moqedalso also paid for his ticket with cash in Baltimore. His choice: seat 12A.

Everything had been planned out, including the seating arrangements.

The nightmare dream of Ramzi Ahmed Yousef, bin Laden's vision of hell, the cataclysmic plans first formulated in 1993 and formalized in 1996, were about to become a horrific reality.

Eight years had passed since the failed attempt on the World Trade Center in 1993.

Five more had elapsed since Abdul Hakim Murad and Ramzi Ahmed Yousef, planned to train and deploy five-man teams that were to hijack American commercial jetliners.

"If we wanted to carry out small operations, it would have been easy to do. The nature of the battle requires good preparation."

— Osama bin Laden

The crown jewel, the ultimate prize was the World Trade Center. To destroy one Tower would be victorious. If both towers were destroyed, it would be an unparalleled triumph in the world of terrorism.

The stakes were high.

The odds uncertain.

Every precaution had been taken.

The terrorists would go to any length to insure victory and victory required that at least one tower should fall.

Atta was the field commander and the general and to him the honor should fall. Extra-precautions were taken to insure that at least one jet, the one piloted by Atta, would be successfully hijacked and slammed into the World Trade Center.

They were going to take no chances and made sure they would be able to circumvent the lax security at Logan Airport.

The solution was simple.

They would avoid it altogether.

The plan called for Atta and Alomari to rent a car in Boston, drive to Portland, Maine, and then check in at the much smaller airport in Portland where security was believed to be especially lax during the early morning hours. From Portland they would catch a connecting flight to California, Flight 11.

Flight 11 was also to have the most pilots.

Three of the five hijackers on Flight 11 had flight training and at least two of those on Flight 175 had been trained as pilots. Flight 175 was to strike the second tower.

Multiple pilots insured that if one or even two of their team were killed, injured or incapacitated, at least one of the remaining hijackers would be able to fulfill their deadly mission.

Of the four flights to be hijacked that day, the success of those targeting the Pentagon and the White House were considered to be of lesser importance.

The plane to be commandeered by Ziad Jarrahi and his team, Flight 93, consisted of only 4 hijackers: Saeed Alghamdi, Ahmed Alhaznawi, and Ahmed Alnami—though it is possible that one additional hijacker had second thoughts and abandoned the mission at the last moment.

******

As August became September and the designated day for the hijacking neared, the terrorists began a mass migration. The plot was in play.

Abdulaziz Alomari who had lived in a rented a home with his wife and four children moved out on September 3. Although he sent his family back to Saudi Arabia, he had no plans to leave the country.

He was to join Atta.

Atta and Alomari drove to Boston in Atta's flaming red Pontiac. They parked it in the lot at Logan International Airport and caught a flight to Canada, apparently making contact with a female agent that was living there. Next, they traveled to Maine in order to confer with other terrorists who were gathering there.

Hani Hanjour, Khalid Al-Midhar, Majed Moqed, Nawaq Alhamzi, and Salem Alhamzi, who were to hijack Flight 77 and slam it into the Pentagon, set up housekeeping in Washington. Over the following days they made several dry runs. Hani Hanjour even paid an instructor at Freeway Airport in Bowie to guide him on three flights over the Washington area.

Hani and his team also joined a gym and during the days leading up to the greatest terrorist tragedy in American history, they spent their free time lifting weights at Gold's Gym in Greenbelt. Three of the men even bought temporary membership.

Likewise, the others were on the move and began to assemble and rent motel rooms close to the targeted airports, Ronald Reagan International Airport, Boston's Logan Airport and the Newark International Airport in New Jersey.

Once assembled near the targeted airports some of them would take flights on the same commercial jets that days later, they would hijack—preparing themselves by taking trial runs.

******

In the months leading up to September, although many of the men had congregated in Florida, not all the hijackers had been living within easy commuting distance.

Some had been staying in Cambridge and Salem Massachusetts, and, in Los Angeles and San Diego California. Others may have resided in Canada, as well as briefly in Arizona and Virginia.

Yet, it was necessary for them to communicate.

The phone was not an option.

Someone might be listening.

The U.S. mail was unreliable.

Someone might open a letter.

The solution?

The Internet.

The hijackers used the Internet not only to purchase plane tickets but to keep in constant communication. The internet appears to have been the primary vehicle they relied on most to coordinate their movements during the final days, hours and minutes leading up to the moment they boarded the four doomed flights.

As the final day approached, there was an increasing need for the conspirators to stay in contact.

Atta and some of his coconspirators headed to the nearest Internet Cafe, in this case, one located in Bangor, Maine.

Owner, Stephen Stimpson recalled that they asked to rent two computers.

They said they needed to check their e-mails. They had a hotmail.com e-mail account.

One of the men printed out his messages. Then he typed in his reply.

The two brothers, Waleed M. Alshehri and Wail Alshehri were also on the move. Like the others, Waleed M. Alshehri and Wail had an e-mail account. Theirs was with Net.Zero.

According to the FBI, Mohald Alshehri was among the hijackers who seized United Airlines Flight 175, which crashed into the World Trade Center's south tower. The other two

Alshehris, Waleed M. Alshehri and Wail Alshehri, were on Flight 11, which hit the north tower.

As they journeyed to their date with destiny, the Alsheri brothers would stop off at local libraries or rent motel rooms that provided Internet access.

They had to check their e-mails.

They were on a mission from god.

In early September, Waleed M. Alshehri and Wail stopped off at the public library in Delray Beach. They did not apply for a library card and did not check out any books.

They needed to access the Internet.

They had to check their messages.

They said they received a lot of e-mail.

Katherine Hensman, the research librarian in Delray Beach, remembered the two men. After the suicide hijackings, she contacted the FBI.

The Alshehri brothers, checked into a local motel after being assured it offered internet access.

They had to check their messages.

They said they received a lot of e-mails.

A third man joined them an hour later. He too had to check his messages.

Paul Dragomir, who runs the Longshore motel, in Hollywood, Florida, remembered the men and also notified the FBI.

As recalled by Dragomir, the three men showed up with a lot of baggage and said they had to have 24-hour Internet access and they had to have it in their room. Dragomir said he would see what he could do.

Satisfied, the three men retired for some sun and fun on the beach. While they were gone a woman from Canada called and inquired about them.

After they returned several hours later Dragomir informed them he could not provide 24-hour Internet access in their room.

The men were enraged.

They were angry.

"You don't understand. We're on a mission," they said.
Their mission was mass murder.

******

On the evening of September 10, Atta drove to Boston in his red Pontiac and left it in the airport parking lot. He and Abdul Alomari then rented a car at the Logan Airport Alamo and drove to Maine

Two other hijackers rented their vehicle, a white Mitsubishi, from the same Alamo franchise.

Although Atta had repeatedly practiced this operation, on the morning of September 11, he was so worried that he might miss his flight from Maine to Boston that he rushed out and forgot his luggage. Later FBI agents would discover a jet fuel consumption calculator, an instructional video on flying commercial jets, a scrap of lined paper with a list of helpful hijacker hints, a letter, dated from 1996, and a kind of Hijacker's epistle.

In the notes and letter he left behind, Atta said he planned to kill himself so he would go to heaven as a martyr.

He also wrote out a page of last minute reminders which he may have photocopied and circulated among his followers. Atta, the presume author, had doodled on the paper, sketching a crude "key of life" that consisted of a arrowhead-like sword, with serpentine swirls and two hoops circling the shaft.

The letter also said in part:

"It is a raid for Allah....When the time of truth comes and zero hour arrives, then straighten out your clothes, open your heart and welcome death for the sake of Allah. Seconds before the target, your last words should be: There is no God but Allah. Mohammed is his messenger. I pray to you, God, to forgive me from all my sins, to allow me to glorify you in every possible way."

The FBI also found a detailed letter, a kind of Hijacker's Epistle which had apparently been circulated among all four hijacker teams, for a copy was also found in the debris of yet another hijacked jetliner.

It read in part as follows:

"In the name of God, the most merciful, the most compassionate. . . . In the name of God, of myself and of my family . . . I pray to you God to forgive me from all my sins, to allow me to glorify you in every possible way..."

"Remember the battle of the prophet . . . against the infidels, as he went on building the Islamic state..."

And then, on the top of page 3, it was captioned:

"The last night."

"Remind yourself that in this night you will face many challenges. But you have to face them and understand it 100 percent."

"Obey God, his messenger, and don't fight among yourself where you become weak, and stand fast, God will stand with those who stood fast."

"You should engage in such things, you should pray, you should fast. You should ask God for guidance, you should ask God for help. . . . Continue to pray throughout this night. Continue to recite the Koran."

"Purify your heart and clean it from all earthly matters. The time of fun and waste has gone. The time of judgment has arrived. Hence we need to utilize those few hours to ask God for forgiveness. You have to be convinced that those few hours that are left you in your life are very few. From there you will begin to live the happy life, the infinite paradise. Be optimistic. The prophet was always optimistic."

"Always remember the verses that you would wish for death before you meet it if you only know what the reward after death will be."

"Everybody hates death, fears death. But only those, the believers who know the life after death and the reward after death, would be the ones who will be seeking death."

"Remember the verse that if God supports you, no one will be able to defeat you."

"Keep a very open mind, keep a very open heart of what you are to face. You will be entering paradise. You will be entering the happiest life, everlasting life. Keep in your mind that if you are plagued with a problem and how to get out of it. A believer is always plagued with problems. . . . You will never enter paradise if you have not had a major problem. But only those who stood fast through it are the ones who will overcome it."

"Check all of your items, your bag, your clothes, knives, your will, your IDs, your passport, all your papers. Check your safety before you leave. . . . Make sure that nobody is following you. . . . Make sure that you are clean, your clothes are clean, including your shoes."

"In the morning, try to pray the morning prayer with an open heart. Don't leave but when you have washed for the prayer. Continue to pray."

"When you arrive ... smile and rest assured, for Allah is with the believers and the angels are protecting you."

"When you enter the plane pray:

"Oh God, open all doors for me. Oh God who answers prayers and answers those who ask you, I am asking you for your help. I am asking you for forgiveness. I am asking you to lighten my way. I am asking you to lift the burden I feel."

"Oh God, you who open all doors, please open all doors for me, open all venues for me, open all avenues for me."

"God, I trust in you. God, I lay myself in your hands. I ask with the light of your faith that has lit the whole world and lightened all darkness on this earth, to guide me until you approve of me. And once you do, that's my ultimate goal."

"There is no God but God. There is no God who is the God of the highest throne, there is no God but God, the God of all earth and skies. There is no God but God, I being a sinner. We are of God, and to God we return."

******

On the morning of September 11, Mohamed Atta and Abdulaziz Alomari, caught a flight departing Portland, Maine, which had a connecting flight in Boston.

Atta and Alomari were in fact videotaped at the Portland Jetport boarding a 6 a.m. flight for Boston.

The connecting flight was American Airlines Flight 11. Later that same morning, Flight 11 would slam into the north Tower of the World Trade Center.

Some of the other terrorists had been in Massachusetts for days, having rented rooms in various cities located within driving distance of Boston's Logan International Airport. In fact, two of the hijackers, Ahmed Alghamdi and Saeed Alghamdi listed Massachusetts as their official residence and had obtained Massachusetts drivers licenses.

In the days before the attack, a rental car used by five of the hijackers had been picked up by surveillance videos, driving in and then later out of the airport, five different times.

One of the men in the car was Marwan Al-Shehhi. He and his team had rented motel rooms near the airport. Al-Shehhi and at least one other of the men spent their last evening at the Panther Motel Apartments in Boston.

Al-Shehhi, like Atta was afraid he would miss his flight. On the morning of September 11, in his haste to catch his plane, he left behind a stack of aeronautical maps of the East Coast and a box cutter.

Marwan Al-Shehhi, accompanied by his four men, hurried to Boston's Logan International Airport in a Mitsubishi sedan rented from National Car Rentaland. They exited the vehicle and walked rapidly toward the boarding gates, their performance recorded by surveillance cameras.

They were in such a hurry to catch their flight, they left something very interesting behind. Flight manuals.

******

They were now ready for the final act. Weaknesses in security and defense had been detailed, studied and documented, targets were identified, and over the course of the next two hours they would commit the most horrific, brazen and well-planned terrorist attacks in American history.

The attack would be unprecedented in scope and sophistication. The coordinated assault on America's political, military and financial capital would wreak havoc and catch the United States government completely off guard — despite a massive law enforcement and intelligence network which exist solely to detect and thwart such attacks.

The American government would be completely unprepared for the possibility that jetliners would be hijacked for the purpose of being used as fuel-laden guided missiles.

By the evening of September 11, 2001, the United States would never again be the same.

America Attacked

America Attacked

America Attacked

America Attacked

America Attacked

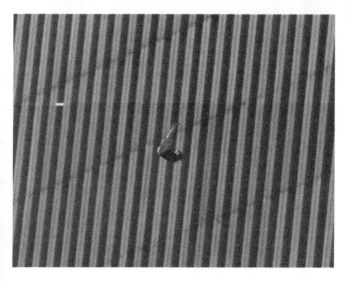

America Attacked

America Attacked

AMERICAN AIRLINES FLIGHT 11

The terrorists had been well trained. To overcome the disadvantage of racial profiling and the possibility of drawing attention to themselves, they had been taught to think only pleasant thoughts, to visualize pleasant memories...the face of a loved one, a sexual encounter...

No one standing in line to board American Airlines Flight 11 probably paid the men much attention. The possibility of a hijacking might not have occurred to anyone. Whatever fears, anxieties or apprehensions experienced by the passengers or crew would have probably been limited to the uncertainties associated with takeoffs and landings. This is when most airline accidents occur.

American Airlines Flight 11, scheduled to leave Boston's Logan Airport, en route for Los Angeles, at 7:58 A.M. began much the same as the thousands of other departures. If anyone had suggested that knife welding hijackers would crash the plane into the World Trade Center, it would have been treated as a perverse and absurd joke.

There were 81 passengers on board. Five of them, including Mohamed Atta, knew that what would happen next would be no joke. The terrorists took up their positions and like crouching tigers, waited for the right moment to leap upon and disarm their prey.

They had rehearsed the operation a hundred times until the well-choreographed routine became second nature. The men would brandish makeshift knives created from shaving supplies and razor blades. The female flight attendants would be threatened and forced to the back of the plane. Once the pilots opened the cockpit door to intervene, the hijackers would rush in, take control, and switch off the alarms that would alert ground control that something was amiss.

The pilots, whose training emphasized that hijackings should not be resisted, would be tied up with nylon rope. This would insure they could not fight back when the terrorists began stabbing them to death.

Eliminating the pilots was a key element in their plan.

No pilot, even with a gun at his head, would steer his craft into a building packed with women and men—which is why the terrorists had trained as pilots: to do what would never come natural to a natural man.

The pilots had to be killed, at least in the mind of the hijacker's fevered brain, so as to eliminate the possibility that they might get free and intervene and put a stop to this monstrous plan.

The pilots would be tied up and killed.

Atta had booked his reservation two weeks in advance, paying for a one-way First Class, Business Section ticket on American Airlines Flight 11. The jet was a Boeing 767, a plane Atta had been trained to fly and maneuver. Atta was assigned to seat 8D, just a few short steps from the cockpit.

One of Atta's bags somehow missed the flight. Later, when the FBI opened and examined the contents of this bag, they found airline uniforms, a video on commercial aircraft, and a suicide note dated 1996—indicating that the attack had been planned five years earlier.

Atta had also paid for the ticket of Abdulaziz Alomari, who traveled on the same flight. Alomari was assigned to seat 3C. Alomari, and the three other hijackers, had their own roles to play. They would kill a stewardess as a diversion, and then the pilots.

The jet departed from Boston at 7:58 a.m. It was right on time. Forty seven minutes later, it would crash into the north Tower of New York's World Trade Center.

Abdul Alomari waited for the signal. There were 8 flight attendants on board. If he wanted, he could have read their ID tags and committed their names to memory. There was Barbara Arestegui, Jeffrey Collman, Sara Low, Karen Martin, Kathleen Nicosia, Betty Ong, Jean Roger, Dianne Snyder, and Madeline Sweeney. But it was the pilots he was most concerned about.

John Ogonowski was the pilot. Tom McGuinness, the co-pilot, was his second in command.

Everyone liked John Ogonowski. He had just celebrated his 52 birthday with his wife and three daughters, Laura, 16; Caroline, 14; and Mary Catherine, 11. He was also a farmer who loved to work the land. He dreamed of retiring on his 150-acre property.

There were also a few "celebrities" on board the doomed plane, including David Angell the executive producer of NBC's hit television show "Frasier." Angell had also written episodes for shows such as "Wings" and "Cheers," and won six Emmy Awards for his television work. Atta, who would soon hijack the plane, sat across from him.

David and his wife, Lynn, were flying back to their home in Pasadena. They were returning from their summer home in Chatham, Massachusetts, where they had just celebrated the wedding of a family member.

There was also an actress on the flight, Berry Berenson. She had appeared in a number of movies including ''Cat People,'' ''Winter Kills'' and ''Remember My Name.'' She was the widow of actor Anthony Perkins who achieved fame as the serial killer "Norman Bates" in Alfred Hitchcock's "Psycho."

A billionaire was also on board American Airlines Flight 11. Daniel C. Lewin, 31, who attended graduate school at MIT, was co-founder of Akamai Technologies. Lewin became an instant billionaire during the firm's October 1999 initial public offering, when the company made an impressive Wall Street debut.

Carolyn Beug and her mother Mary Alice Wahlstrom were seated together. Carolyn was a noted Santa Monica filmmaker and music video producer and had won an award for her work on the Van Halen video "Right Now." She also loved to write and was working on a children's novel, detailing the story of

Noah's Ark, told from the point of view of Noah's wife.

Carolyn was also a "cheerleader" for the girl's track team at Santa Monica High School. Her twin daughters, Lauren and Lindsey Mayer-Beug, 18, had been the team's captains. Carolyn would have done anything for her daughters, including, as she had done that week, escorting them to college, where they were starting their first year at Rhode Island School of Design. Mission accomplished, Carolyn and her own mother, were headed to home sweet home.

A refugee from the horrors of the U.S.-backed right wing death squads of El Salvador, Gloria de Barrera, 49, had also taken this flight. Gloria and her family had moved to the U.S., in 1980, to flee the civil wars. She had gone to school, taught herself English, this girl from a small village in El Salvador, and had made a success of her life as an exporter. She came to America in search of freedom, and was living the American dream.

In a few moments, the "fighters of freedom" would turn that dream into a nightmare.

Seven young business women had also caught this flight, Christine Barbuto, 32, Neilie Casey, 32, Tara Creamer, 30, Lisa Gordenstein, 41, Linda George, 27, Robin Kaplan, 33, and Susan MacKay, 42. Hip, professional, laughing and joking, they were close friends and colleagues, and sitting together in adjacent seats. All worked for T.J. Maxx and often traveled around the country to take care of business at different stores.

But on this trip, they had more on their mind than just business. Linda George was engaged, she was to be married that very month. The women may well have been laughing and kidding and discussing her marriage plans, when the hijackers struck.

There was a rock musician on board, Danny Lee. Danny Lee was also a "roadie" for the band, the Back Street Boys. Danny had just finished a big concert Monday night, but instead of sticking around for the next one, he had decided to head home to be with his wife, who was pregnant. The baby was due the next day and he wanted to be with her when the baby was born. Danny had only gotten a few hours sleep, but he made it to the airport bright and early. He was determined to see his little girl get born, and to be with the woman he loved. It was not to be.

There was also an astronaut on board, Charles "Chuck" Jones, 48. He had been qualified to fly on the space shuttle, but the 1987 Challenger explosion indefinitely postponed launches and put an end to his dream.

Laurie Naneira, 49, had hoped to take this flight with her daughter, Francisca, 31. It was a discounted plane ticket, which made all the difference between life and death.

Because her husband, Gil, was a technician for American Airlines, Laurie had a deeply discounted ticket on Flight 11.

Francisca's husband worked for Delta and she held a discount ticket on a Delta flight.

They boarded separate flights to Los Angeles, which departed a few minutes apart. They had planned to meet five hours later. Instead, 45 minutes later, Francisca's plane would be diverted to Cleveland, where she would learn that her mother's plane had crashed into the north Tower of the World Trade Center.

Laurie Naneira, Carolyn, David and Lynn Angell, Berry Berenson, Daniel Lewin and the other passengers, including Sonia Morales Puopolo, a former ballet dancer, and Peter Gay, Vice President and General Manager of Raytheon, all settled in for what they expected would be a routine flight.

It would be anything but that.

Flight 11 took off at 7:59 am and began traveling along its normal route west. Then, something went wrong.

The big jet had been instructed by air traffic controllers to climb to 31,000 feet. Yet the pilot failed to respond.

"He was cleared to continue his climb, and he did not," said one controller. "I issued instructions again, but he didn't respond. Now I knew there was a problem."

"Again, I issued instructions to climb."

There was still no response.

A few moments later, air traffic controllers began receiving desperate messages over an open mike. American Airlines Flight 11 had been hijacked and an Arab terrorist was in the cockpit threatening the pilot's life.

"Don't do anything foolish. You're not going to get hurt," the heavily accented voice said to the pilot.

Unbeknownst to the terrorist, the pilot was repeatedly and intermittently triggering a radio microphone in the cockpit.

According to an unidentified controller in Nashua, NH, who was handling the flight: "When he pushed the button and the terrorist spoke, we knew there was a terrible problem. There was this heavily accented voice that was threatening the pilot. He was clearly very threatening."   The controller also heard someone in the cockpit telling the pilot that, "We have more planes, we have other planes."

The radio microphone went dead.

The jet was over central New York, 17 miles southwest of Albany, when, according to radar tracking data, it suddenly turned abruptly to the south. It was at that moment, about 30-minutes into the flight that the jet's transponder was turned off.

The jet began flying erratically, accelerating and then decelerating, slowing and then speeding up from its normal cruising speed. It slowed to cruising speed again as the jet followed the Hudson River into Manhattan.

Within a few minutes, it would hit the north tower of the World Trade Center.

******

A camera crew was waiting for them. A group of Islamic militants had set up camera and videotaping equipment on a rooftop in Union City, New Jersey. They had a perfect view of the Twin Towers. Now, all they had to do was wait.

The cameras were already rolling. In a few minutes, they would videotape Flight 11 and then Flight 175 as they slammed into the World Trade Center. They would continue to videotape as the Twin Towers imploded.

As the first of the doomed jets struck the gleaming super-structures, they began to cheer.

A few hours later, the National Security Agency would intercept a cell phone call from the United States to a suspected bin Laden operative in Europe.

The message was short and to the point: "We hit the targets."

8:48 A.M. THE NORTH TOWER OF THE WORLD TRADE CENTER

******

8:48 a.m. American Airlines Flight 11, a Boeing 767 en route from Boston's Logan Airport to Los Angeles International with 92 people onboard, slams into the north Tower of the World Trade Center.

******

Roko Camaj had been washing the windows of the World Trade Center ever since it opened in 1973. For nearly 20 years, he had been doing what now came naturally: setting up the rigging for the scrubbing machines that washed the windows.

It was 8:44 A.M. and at this height and this hour, it was fairly quiet on the roof. Roko Camaj loved his job. He was enamored by the view.

Roko stood at the top of the world and took it all in. Wisps of clouds swirled overhead and there was the breathtaking city skyline and the harbor below.

All seemed peaceful. He was on top of the world.

Perhaps he saw it. Maybe he heard it: in the distance, a Boeing 767, coming closer, following the path of the Hudson river into the heart of Manhattan.

Then, the sound of its engines grew into a roar.

Roko stopped working and looked down in amazement.

The jet was way too low. It wasn't flying level, but with its right wing crazily tilted skyward and the left wing angled towards the ground. It looked like a giant gleaming blade that was about to slice into the North Tower.

And then it struck. There was a sickening explosion and the building began to rock.

Hundreds of people were instantly incinerated. Those on the floors above were enveloped in flames.

Smoke began billowing out of the wounded tower and into the floors above.

Roko called his wife on his cell phone. He told her what had happened. He said he was going to take the stairwell down.

But there was no way down. The floors below and the stairwells were engulfed in flames.

He climbed back up, seeking safety. He called his wife again.

He would wait on the roof with the others that escaped the blazing inferno below. He said that he would wait for a rescue helicopter.

Roko would never be seen or heard from again.

Over 400 people were at work that morning at Marsh USA Inc. Marsh was a risk management and insurance firm that occupied the 93rd through 100th floors.

It was business as usual. Employees were checking their e-mails, making phone calls, talking to one another, having coffee and making jokes.

Perhaps almost everybody heard it coming—heard that unusual sound: the roaring of a jet engine. Those who looked up and gazed through the windows saw the oddly angled jet headed right towards them.

Most of them didn't have a chance.

Later that day, Marsh USA Inc., would report that 400 of their workers were missing.

American Airline Flight 11, struck the northwest corner of the 91st floor of the north Tower at precisely 8:48 a.m. The twelve employees of the American Bureau of Shipping, a nonprofit group that promotes safety and property protection at sea, were directly in the airplane's path of destruction. They were instantly obliterated.

Also killed instantly were the employees in the office above them. The jet's right wing, angled toward the sky, had sliced right through their floor.

As the bulk of the plane's fuselage slammed into the 91st floor, there was a massive explosion, which ripped through several of the upper and lower levels. Hundreds of men and women were instantly incinerated. Many of those who escaped the flames fell from the windows to their deaths.

Some fell because they were disoriented by the blast and because they couldn't see where they were going from all the smoke. Some were blown through gaping windows by the force of the blast. Others, hysterical and frantically backing away from the 2000 degree heat, leapt to escape the unbearable temperatures, plummeting to the ground below.

Tom McGinnis was attending a brokerage meeting on the 92nd floor when the jet slammed into the North Tower. There was a tremendous explosion. The walls collapsed and the building shook and swayed. Billowing white smoke began to pour into the wrecked offices. He turned towards the windows and could see people falling or jumping from the floors above him.

Tom surveyed the wreckage the billowing smoke and fires, and realized he would be unable to get out alive. Calmly, he called his wife, Iliana, his high school sweetheart and the mother of 4-year-old daughter Caitlin.

"This doesn't look good," he said. "There's no way out of this room. . . . I love you. Take care of Caitlin."

"Don't hang up," Iliana said. "Don't hang up. You are coming home."

He is among the presumed dead.

Andrew Stern, 41, Wendy Small, 26, Amy O'Doherty, 23 and over a thousand other men and women were all employed by the Cantor Fitzgerald International Securities Firm, which occupied floors 101-105 of the north tower.

Wendy was a college graduate and had a 7-year-old son named Tyree. She had been with Cantor Fitzgerald for two years.

Andrew was a bond broker who helped coach his son's Little

League team.

Amy had just moved to New York and into her very first apartment. She had managed to place a call to her mother in the moments after the crash.

But Amy, Wendy, Andrew and a thousand more of their colleagues were never heard from again.

Reuben was waiting outside the conference room on the 105 floor of the North tower, talking to his fiance, Maria, on his cell phone, waiting for the others to arrive and for the meeting to begin.

He glanced at his watch. It was 8:45 a.m.

"I've got to go," he was saying, and then there was a deafening explosion. The floor beneath him buckled upward and Reuben was tossed into the air and then against a collapsing wall.

"Bomb!" somebody screamed.

Reuben freed himself from beneath the rubble and crawled with his cell phone in hand. All the windows around him were shattered. There were shards of glass and debris everywhere. Office memos and documents were swirling through the air and out the broken windows. People were screaming, crying.

Reuben crawled laboriously into the hall and stood up. There was smoke everywhere. It was difficult to breathe. Everything was hot, unbearably hot. He had to get out. The elevator doors opened and several people rushed out, their bodies in flames.

Reuben ran toward the stairwell. In his right hand he still gripped his cell phone As he descended the stairs he hit redial and called his fiance.

"There's been an explosion. A bomb. But I'm O.K." he said.

There were other people in the stairwell. Many were burnt and bloody. But they were heading up, not down.

"There's no way down," someone said. "We have to get on the roof and wait for a rescue helicopter."

"I'm going to the roof," Reuben told his fiance: "I've got to go. I love you."

"I love you," she replied.

Maria never saw Reuben again.

George Sleigh had been sitting in his cubicle since 7:30 a.m.

"I heard this unusual sound. A roaring sound," he said. "As I looked up I saw the plane. I thought: "This guy is really low.""

"It was coming right at us. A wing flashed past my eyes and for a brief moment I could see the plane's smooth belly. Then the world caved in and I was buried alive in ceiling tiles, book-shelves and technical manuals."

Offices down the hall and on the floors above were obliterated.

"Some of my colleagues dug me out and we all escaped."

George Sleigh would be one of the "lucky ones."

It was pandemonium and total confusion for the occupants and visitors on the 87th Floor. Suffocating white smoke was fill-ing the hallways and liquid sparks were snaking along the floor — it was the jet fuel that had not exploded.

Many people, like those on the floors above, succumbed to the smoke and heat.

Those who were able to escape from the upper floors quickly filed down the stairwell and then opened the door to the 78th floor, which contained a transfer lobby where one set of eleva-tors and stairs ended and another set of stairs and elevators be-gan. The 78th floor had erupted in a wall of flames.

Some people, in their haste to escape, ran to the elevators. Those who chose what they hoped would be the quickest way down, were never seen again. Many of them went down in a free fall to their deaths or were engulfed in jet fuel and set aflame.

Arlene Charles and Carmen Griffith were working on the 78th floor that morning. Carmen's husband, Arturo operated the freight elevator in the same building. He would later escape with a broken leg.

It was the job of both Arlene and Carmen to turn on the elevators and to ferry tourists to the famed Windows on the World restaurant, located at the top of the North Tower.

Arlene was standing in the lobby when the jet hit. She was thrown to the floor. Smoke and flame filled the halls. And then there were the agonizing screams.

Burning jet fuel erupted through the elevator doors and engulfed Carmen. She had been standing next to the elevator when the jet hit. Carmen was on fire, her skin peeling from her face and hands.

The elevators were a burning death trap. There was only one way out. Down the stairs.

******

"I had been sitting in my office on the 54th floor, reading e-mails, when an explosion rocked the building. The building began swaying back and forth, to and fro... I thought it was going to fall into the Hudson River."

"Somebody said there had been a bomb and that's what I thought too. I remembered the bombing in 1993."

"I got up and went to the window and could see what looked like confetti: thousands and thousands of shredded sheets of paper were blowing in the wind and drifting down. It was a blizzard of white paper fluttering past our window and down to the ground. Then I saw something bigger and darker quickly drop past the window. I thought, maybe, it was a high backed executive's chair. But then the guy next to me said: 'did you see that? That was a body. A man's body!'"

"We decided to get the hell out of there and rushed into the corridor and then into the emergency staircase. It was smoky inside and it smelled like diesel fuel. There were other people coming down the stairs. Some were badly burnt: no hair, no eyebrows and their clothes singed and smoking. There was a woman whose face was bloody. Her clothes were singed and ragged. Her skin looked red and angry. She had been badly burned. We let her and some of the others who were hurt go ahead of us so they could get help and descend more rapidly."

"As we got to about the 40th floor, it was no longer smoky and the smell was gone, but it was slow going. We had to form a single line and go down single file. Firemen were coming up in the other direction."

The firemen had been out on another call but immediately headed to the World Trade Center when the call came in at around 9:10 am.

"'You're going to be all right,' one of the firemen said."

"That's when I heard the second explosion. Again I could feel the building sway. I thought it was going to collapse at any moment."

"Yet, everybody stayed calm. Nobody knew that a second jet had just hit the south Tower."

"Everyone was in control of themselves. Maybe it was because of the firemen. Here we were trying to get down to save our lives, and these guys were heading up in order to save the lives of those who could not save themselves."

"I almost felt ashamed. These guys are heroes! These guys are supermen. There was no way you could get me to go back up, but these guys...Firemen! These guys were brave!"

"And then I thought: They're all going to die. Every one of these guys. These firemen. They are all going to die and they know it."

"It made me feel sick."

"The noxious, toxic smells disappeared as we got closer to the ground, but as I stepped out into the plaza, I was shocked. Everything was topsy-turvy. The windows and doors were all blown out. The overhead sprinklers had gone off. There were mountains of debris and twisted metal, and everything was covered with ash. There was dust and debris and water and broken glass everywhere."

"I didn't linger. I wanted to get out."

"I stepped outside and froze. There on the ground, I saw a leg, and then an arm, and body parts. Everywhere I looked I could see body parts. It made me sick. I quit looking. I started to run."

Adam, 35, arrived at his office on the 87th floor at 8:30 a.m. He and his colleagues were drinking coffee and checking their email when the building lurched violently. It shook as if there had been an earthquake and seemed to sway five or more feet in each direction. It did not occur to anyone that the building was struck by a plane.

Parts of the ceiling started to collapse and smoke began billowing in through the gaps. Glancing out the window, Adam saw paper flying everywhere, like the New York Yankee's ticker tape parade. The building was still rumbling and shaking. Fearful of being hurt by falling debris, Adam and a colleague ducked beneath a doorway. They were quite sure it had been a bomb.

Adam and his colleagues, 13 people in all, thought the worst was over. The building was standing and they were shaken but alive. Adam stepped into the hall. It was filling with thick white smoke but it smelled unusual, unlike a barbecue, a fireplace or a bonfire.

To his surprise, the phones were still working. Adam called his nanny at home and told her to page his wife and tell her that a bomb had gone off but they were all fine and on their way out.

But things were not fine. He had spoke too soon.

The thick smoke was making it harder to breath. It was also getting hotter.

Fire!

Adam ripped his shirt into several pieces. He soaked them in water and gave 2 pieces to his friends. They wrapped the wet rags around their faces and headed towards the stair well. There were tiny fires and sparks in the halls.

One of his friends hesitated. It would be safer, he said, if they waited for the police or fire department to come and get them. Adam disagreed but his friend decided to stay back.

Adam descended to the 85th floor and then realized that his friend would die if they left him behind. He and an associate climbed back up the two flights through a fog of smoke.

Desperately, Adam began calling his friend's name over and over. They checked through the office. There was no response.

The situation was rapidly deteriorating. They made haste.

Adam and his coworker again descended the stairwell. On the 78th floor they had to switch to a different stairwell, but as they entered the lobby there was a wall of flames. Someone was trying to fight the fire with an emergency hose. It was a losing proposition.

They all moved gingerly down Stair Case A. The evacuation was slow, but orderly and there were no signs of panic. Adam's legs were shaking and his heart seemed to be in his throat. He checked his cell phone. Surprisingly there was a strong signal. He called his parents and told them he was okay and on his way down.

On the 53rd floor, Adam came across a heavy set man who looked shell shocked and in no position to move. He refused all offers of help and decided to wait for the rescue workers.

"It was on the 44th floor that we first saw firemen, policemen, WTC K-9 units without dogs and just about anyone with a badge heading upwards." Adam was almost out the building at the 3rd floor when the lights went out. Everything went black as they heard a rumbling coming toward them from above. It was the South Tower collapsing right next door.

Someone had a flashlight. Adam and the others headed down a dark and cramped corridor to an exit. It was pitch black. Impossible to see. Blindly, holding on to one another for support, they slowly descended the stairwell and in the wavering beam of the flashlight, they saw a female police officer emerge soaking wet and covered in soot.

She was obviously upset, but she kept her cool.

The exit was completely blocked, she told them. And then pointed them in another direction. She stayed behind to guide those still emerging from the stairwell.

She would never get out alive.

Finally, they stepped out into the courtyard where the fountain used to be. Twisted steel and wires jutted out everywhere, and everywhere and everything was covered by pasty dusty drywall soot.

Where was everybody?

Adam and the others gazed at the destruction all around them in shock. Then shock was followed by horror.

They saw the body parts. A leg, an arm, a burnt torso, a hand that stretched out from beneath the twisted mountain of debris.

Adam realized he was looking at the bodies of the rescue workers, and those of his friends and colleagues who had got out just minutes before him.

"If I hadn't gone back to get my friend, I would have been stepping outside just as the south tower fell. I would have died too."

"It was horrible. It was all so horrible. "

Several blocks away they stopped and sat down. A girl on a bike offered them some water. Just as she took the lid off her bottle, they heard a rumble. Tower 1 was collapsing. They had been out less than 15 minutes.

******

Stunned observers witnessed people falling from the upper floors of the north tower. It was a surreal, horrifying sight to behold.

James Braddock had just stepped outside from the Federal Post Office Building across the street from the World Trade Center.

"I heard this incredibly loud explosion. By reflex, I ducked down, because it sounded like it was right on top of me. When I glanced up, there was all this debris and stuff, falling from the sky, falling from the Trade Center. The first thing I thought was that a huge bomb must have gone off."

"Other people were standing on the sidewalk looking up and pointing. I squinted my eyes. I couldn't believe it. There were people falling from the sky. They were either jumping or maybe the force of the explosion threw them out. More and more people started flying out of the top floors: Men in suits, women in dresses...falling, falling."

Candice Porter had just exited a cab across the street from the World Trade Center, when she caught the sound of a jet plane.

"I had worked as a flight attendant for almost five years so I knew that sound. I also knew that something was wrong. What was it doing flying so low in the middle of Manhattan? I looked up. I didn't see the plane, but I saw the explosion."

"All at once, all this paper began to stream toward the ground. Paper everywhere. Then the smoke starting billowing out, forming a huge black towering cloud.

"Suddenly people on the sidewalk began yelling: 'Oh my god! They're jumping! They're jumping out the windows!' Fire was shooting out of the building and people were leaping from the top floors. They were tumbling out, one after another. I saw a man and a woman holding hands as they fell."

"I couldn't understand why they were jumping. Why were they doing that? It made me ill. I had to turn away."

Ruby Lopez exited the Manhattan subway just after the first plane hit the north Tower of the World Trade Center.

"I looked up and could see fire, smoke and lots and lots of sheets of papers. So I knew there had been an explosion. I could see fire actually shooting out of the top floors of the building. I could see fire in the upper windows. Fire and smoke. Lots and lots of smoke."

"A woman next to me let out a gasp and grabbed my arm. 'Look!' she yelled. I looked where she was pointing. People were jumping out of the building. Leaping and falling, one after another — sometimes two or even three at a time. I think some of them must have been on fire. But the others? I don't know. It made me very sad."

Firefighter Paul Curran of New York Fire Patrol 3, also saw a lot of people leap from the building. "I don't know how many jumped out and how many were sucked out. But standard aviation fuel is rated to produce incredible heat: 1500 degrees Fahrenheit. When those top floors collapsed, they must have formed shaft-like chimneys, allowing a horrific amount of heat to penetrate the upper and lower floors.

"I don't know what it was like up there but it must have been hell. There were a lot of jumpers. I saw bodies hit the upper level concrete of the second floor overhang of Tower One. Others were falling into West Street."

John Carson, an investment banker couldn't believe his eyes.

"I saw six people fall in the space of 10 minutes. They were somersaulting. People in blue jeans, tennis shoes, business suits, some with no shirts on... falling over themselves, falling."

Jesse Hernandez witnessed the carnage from the 30th floor of a nearby building. "It was a raging inferno. Angry red flames billowing out of the side of the building. You could see windows on the west side popping out and exploding. There were flames licking both sides of the building. I kept thinking of all those people. There must be 5000 people in there! How could anybody survive that?"

"Then, I saw the other plane. A midsize commercial jet. It looked like it was going to slam right into the towers. And it did."

Robert Dickins had just stepped out of the elevator on the 63rd floor of the south tower when Flight 11 struck the north tower. "You could hear it plain as day, a big explosion. I could even smell smoke. Suddenly, even though it was the other tower, everybody started to panic. There was screaming, yelling. People running for the stairwells. It was mass hysteria."

"I didn't see any reason to panic, though I did feel a bit uneasy. I went over to the big window and looked out. The upper floors of the north tower were engulfed in thick black smoke. I could see flames. Tongues of flame and smoke were billowing out of the side of the building."

"As I continued to watch, trying to figure out what happened, I started to see people gathering at some of the broken windows. Smoke was billowing out behind them. Some had ripped off their shirts. They were standing on the sills, or hanging head down over the edge, trying to breath I guess, trying to escape the smoke and the flames behind them. There were dozens and dozens of them, crowded together, some right on top of the others. Leaning out, trying to climb out...trying to get away from the smoke and flames... but there was no place to go."

"Thats when they began leaping out of the top floors. I blinked my eyes. I couldn't believe it. I must have seen a dozen people leaping, or just letting go and dropping like a stone."

"I continued to watch. I was mesmerized. It was surreal, like a bad dream. That's when the second jet hit our building. I immediately ran for the stairwell. I knew I had to get out of there."

UNITED AIRLINES FLIGHT 175

A Boeing 767 is a massive aircraft. The vast majority of Americans could not even conceive of "getting behind the wheel." But Marwan Al-Shehhi had basic flying skills and three hours of flight simulator training to familiarize himself with the layout of the cockpit and the location of the navigation systems.

Given that Marwan wanted only to crash the jet into the World Trade Center and had no interest in any complicated maneuvers, it wasn't necessary for him to know how to work the gears or wing flaps. And as to the rudders, they are controlled automatically by the yaw damper. To fly through the air and to keep the jet airborne, a novice pilot need only know how to work the joystick to climb or bank and how to adjust the throttles.

Taking off and landing, however, takes considerable skill. Al-Shehhi had no intention of landing.

Al-Shehhi took his seat, in the first class business section. He kept his eyes trained on the cockpit door.

The pilot, Victor Saracini 51, of Lower Makefield Township, Pennsylvania, went through a final systems check with the flight engineer and his copilot, Michael Horrocks.

The flight attendants: Amy Jarret, Amy King, Kathryn Laborie, Alfred March and Alan Ogordo, Michael Tarrou and Alicia Titus, went about their duties of reassuring nervous passengers while helping others store their bags.

Garnet "Ace" Bailey, 53, of Lynnfield, Massachusetts and Mark Bavis, 31, took adjoining seats and talked about hockey. "Ace" was director of pro-scouting for the Los Angeles Kings. This would be his 32nd season as a player or scout in the National Hockey League. Before taking on the role of director of pro-scouting for the Kings, Bailey spent 13 years as an Edmonton Oilers scout. The team won five Stanley Cups during that time.

"Ace" was a highly valued professional, with a keen eye for

talent. This would be his eighth year with the Kings.

This was to be Mark's second year as a scout for the Los Angeles Kings. His specialty was recognizing talent in college players. Hockey was in his blood and love of the game ran in the family. His twin brother, Michael, was an assistant coach for Boston University's hockey team.

Heinrich Kimmig, 43, Klaus Bothe, 31, and Wolfgang Menzel, 60, also sat together, speaking quietly in German. Heinrich Kimmig, was Chairman of BCT Technology AG, Germany. Klaus Bothe was Chief of Development and Wolfgang Menzel, Senior Personnel Manager. There was a lot of business to discuss onboard the plane, since important meetings were on the horizon.

Lisa Frost, 22, of Rancho Santa Margarita, California was chatting with a fellow passenger. Lisa was happy and excited. After four grueling years as a student, she was finally returning home to California. Pretty, personable and incredibly smart, Lisa had just graduated No. 1 in her class at Boston University with degrees in communications and business hospitality and marketing.

For the last three months, Lisa had been employed at a Boston-based food magazine. Her last day at the magazine was Friday and her colleagues had taken her to breakfast that morning. They kidded her about the possibility of launching a San Francisco edition of the magazine. She laughed and said would she think about it. Despite the slowing economy, she already had a new job in San Francisco.

But first, Lisa needed to make a stopover in the south Orange County town of Rancho Santa Margarita. She wanted to spend time with her family before heading north to her new job. She was young and excited to embark on this new chapter of her life. Her life was just beginning.

The hijackers, all men of Middle Eastern descent, took their assigned seats and waited for the signal. Acting in accordance with their training, they reconnoitered and then scanned the faces of their fellow passengers in order to identify and then eliminate, if necessary, anyone who looked as if he or she might try to interfere with their plans.

Alona Abraham may have drawn their attention. Not because she posed a threat, but because she was a Jew. She had lived for the last 30 years in the Israeli port town of Ashdot. This was her first visit to the United States and she was excited. She couldn't believe how differently everything seemed compared to her homeland of Israel. Everything was so calm, beautiful and peaceful. The turmoil and turbulence of living under terror had taken its toll on citizens like Alona. She had been thrilled to visit a country that she had only seen and heard about in newspapers and on television.

As Alona had told her relatives, she was also amazed at the diversity of people, originating from countries all over the world. And yet despite their differences, everyone seemed to get along. People gathered together in restaurants and congregated on the streets, chattering away without worrying about each other's religious or ethnic backgrounds.

It certainly wasn't like this in Israel, a nation guarding against terror and combating fear and racial tensions. The threat of Palestinian suicide bombers and the conflicts between Arab and Jewish citizens were unending and only getting worse.

And then, there was the subtle racism and divisions between the Israeli Jews of European descent, the Asknazim and the darker skinned Sephardic Jews. Racial tensions. Violence. Alona was glad to be in America. She felt safe.

In all probablity, the hijackers probably didn't realize she was a Jew. Alona Abraham did not have the physical traits associated with the Asknazim or the Sephardic Jews. Tall, with stunning black eyes and brown hair, she appeared to be "all Indian." Her family immigrated to Israel in the 1950s from Bombay. By all accounts, she was beautiful. Everyone liked Alona. She was a good woman who radiated warmth and heartfelt generosity. She smiled at the woman sitting next to her and settled in for the long flight.

Alona may have attracted the attention of the hijackers because of her beauty. Touri Bolourchi may have caught their eye because she was Persian, a fellow Arab.

Touri Bolourchi, 69, had been born in Tehran and educated in England. However, right after the Islamic revolution she moved to the United States with her daughters in 1979. She had escaped to be free.

Touri met her husband, Akbar Bolourchi, when she was head nurse at Women's Hospital in Tehran and he was a practicing physician there. After the Islamic revolution, Akbar moved his internal medicine practice from Tehran to Beverly Hills. They had escaped to be free.

Besides being an accomplished nurse, Touri also spoke six languages: Turkish, English, French, Italian, Arabic and Farsi.

Touri settled into her seat, feeling nervous. She didn't like flying. She was afraid of airplanes. Two of her cousins died in commercial airline crashes in Europe and Africa. This time, however, she had made an exception. She had wanted to spend a few weeks with her daughter, Roya Turan and two grandsons. That accomplished, and after a wonderful visit, she was now returning home to California. She was anxious to be back with her husband. After all these years they were still deeply in love.

Touri was from an Islamic county—just like all of the hijackers. They killed her anyway.

After the Islamic revolution in Iran, all known homosexuals were rounded up and killed. Islam considers homosexuality to be an offense to god, punishable by death.

Daniel Brandhorst and Ronald Gamboa were a family. They lived together in a home perched on the lip of a canyon in the Hollywood Hills. The couple had been together for over 14 years and had a 3-year old son whom they adopted as an infant. They were returning from a vacation in Boston and Cape Cod.

Ronald Gamboa was a joker who always had a glint of mischief in his eye. He had a thousand jokes, including those about homosexuals. With a ready supply of wit, Ronald would sometimes make himself the butt of his own jokes. He truly believed that life was to be enjoyed and tried to live his to the fullest.

He and Daniel loved to travel. They had trekked all over the world. Whereas Ronald was always ready to laugh and joke, Daniel tended to be more on the serious side. He was a skilled lawyer and accountant, and wanted to become a professor. This dream, he believed, would soon be coming true.

Sue and Peter Hanson waited patiently for the stewardess to fetch them a baby seat, so their two-year-old Christine Hanson would be safely buckled in for takeoff. They were traveling to California to visit relatives in North Hollywood. This was going to be Sue's first visit to California in four years and she wanted her family to meet Christine, her daughter. Like so many children of Asian immigrant families, it was important for Sue to maintain close family ties. Perhaps it was for that reason, that the entire notion of "family" and family roots deeply interested her. She was, in fact, a trained genealogist.

Sue could hardly contain her anticipation. She had spoken with her family by phone the previous night. When they asked if she craved any special food for her visit, she said, "Everything Korean. Everything." Though born in Pasadena, Sue Kim Hanson spent her early childhood in Korea.

Of course, Sue's Korean heritage wouldn't have mattered to the hijackers. People like Sue, and her daughter, and Touri, and Alona... all these women, all these Americans, they were "enemies" that had to be killed.

Ruth McCourt and her four year old niece, Juliana McCourt were also their enemies. Ruth and her daughter were also the unsuspecting victims of fate, irony and tragedy.

Ruth Clifford McCourt and her niece, Juliana were traveling to Los Angeles. Ruth's brother, Ron Clifford was employed at the World Trade Center. Her plane slammed into the very tower that he was working in.

By yet another bizarre and tragic coincidence, Ruth's best friend, Paige Farley-Hackel of Boston, was on American Airlines

Flight 11, which barreled into the other tower.

McCourt and Hackel had been best friends for more than a decade. They traveled the world together. Both stunningly beautiful, the duo turned heads wherever they went. They gave themselves the nickname, "Soul Sisters."

They had both intended on flying together on Flight 175, but they just couldn't get seats on the same plane. Hackel, 46, departed first, on American Airlines Flight 11. Ruth and Juliana boarded United Airlines Flight 175. Ruth and Paige had planned to rendezvous in Los Angeles.

They would never see each other again.

Sue, Peter and Christina; Ronald and Daniel; Heinrich, Klaus, and Wolfgang; Garnet, Mark, Lisa, Alona, Touri and the other passengers, including John Corcoran a marine engineer who was planning to set sail out of the Port of Los Angeles on a container ship, Maclovio 'Joe' Lopez Jr., a burly construction worker, Dorothy A. Dearaujo who painted canals, boats, shops and homes in bold and intricate watercolors, all these passangers probably paid little attention to the five Arabic men who intended to hijack their plane and hijack and desroy their lives.

As the flight attendants began preparing to serve breakfast, the five hijackers, having armed themselves with knives, began acting out the roles they had repeatedly perfected in play.

Marwan Al-Shehhi waited near the cockpit door as Fayez Ahmed, the two Alghamdi brothers, Ahmed and Hamza and Mohald Alshehri began threatening the stewardesses and then stabbed one of them to death.

A passenger, Peter Hanson called his father in Connecticut:

"Something's wrong with the plane. Oh my God! They've stabbed the air hostess. I think the airplane is being hijacked."

Stabbing one or more of the flight attendants was part of the diversion to lure the pilots outside the cockpit, though if necessary, the ill-protected cockpit could be easily stormed. Cockpit doors are tissue thin.

They stabbed a stewardess, and then another—killing killing killing these women, because they were enemies of Islam—though they had never done the hijackers, Islam, or bin Laden any harm.

Stabbing and killing was a diversion. They threatened to continue killing... they may have continued killing and stabbing women and children and the men in an orgy of blood lust and violence—It was god's will: four year old Juliana was an enemy of Islam. Two year old Christine was an enemy of their people.

By killing the evil Americans, their god, Allah, would welcome them to heaven and paradise.

The door to the cockpit flew open. The pilots were trained to cooperate with hijackers, in the hope of giving the passengers on board a chance for survival. But the terrorists knew that if their mission was to succeed, survival was not negotiable.

The pilots were tied up and then killed. With the pilots out of the way, the possibility that the passengers might rebel was greatly diminished.

Once the pilots were dead, who would fly the plane?

Marwan Al-Shehhi, perhaps aided by one of his comrades, stepped inside to commandeer the big jetliner.

It was loaded with 45 tons of jet fuel—more fuel than would ever be needed to fly from Boston to California. The 45 tons of jet fuel alone completely dwarfed the explosive power of the oil bomb that tore off the face of the Murrah Building in Oklahoma City.

In the hands of Marwan Al-Shehhi, this was no longer a jet, but a 200-ton bomb with the explosive power of a nuclear weapon, enough to kill thousands of men and women, mothers and fathers, daughters and sons, and to bring down one of the towers of the World Trade Center.

Flight 175 made a sudden turn and headed toward Manhattan.

******

Ruth McCourt's brother, Ronald Clifford, had arrived 15 minutes early for a business meeting at the World Trade Center. As he strolled across the lobby, he felt the building shake.

It was 8:45 am American Flight 11, Paige-Hackelís flight had just slammed into the North tower.

Eighteen minutes later, at precisely, 9:03 am as Clifford helped a badly burned woman out of the building, he looked up into the sky and saw another plane-United Flight 175 slam into the south tower. The plane was carrying Ruth and Juliana, his sister and niece.

The upper tower burst into a ball of flames. Ron made a dash for safety.

******

9:03 A.M. THE SOUTH TOWER

9:03 a.m. United Airlines Flight 175, a Boeing 767 enroute from Boston to Los Angeles with 65 people onboard, hits the south tower of the World Trade Center.

10:05 a.m. The south tower, also known as 2 World Trade Center, collapses in a plume of ash and debris.

******

Fabian Soto arrived early that morning. He had been working as a window washer apprentice for three weeks when he was assigned to wipe off the nose prints of tourists from the glass of the 107th floor observation deck. Tourists would usually lean against the glass, entranced by the bird's eye view of New York City, which stretched majestically below them.

There were no tourists there this morning. Fabian was all alone.

A few minutes later, a jet struck the south tower. Fabian was never seen again.

Sydney Tolken had made a special trip that morning to the World Trade Center to meet with a colleague on the 104th floor of the World Trade Center. His briefcase was open, papers laid out and he was discussing his investment plans when the first jet struck the opposite tower. He heard the explosion. Both he and his colleague rushed to the window. There were flames and thick black smoke billowing out from the upper floors. He thought it must have been a bomb.

Sydney called his mother to tell her he was alright. He was in the south tower. Whatever had happened in the north Tower must have been an unfortunate freak accident. Though obviously shaken by what he saw, Sydney figured he was safe. He would finish a few things and then head home.

Sydney never made it home. A few minutes later, the second jet crashed into the south tower.

Gordon Aamoth Jr., an investment banker, was at work on the 104th floor of the World Trade Center. He too called home and spoke with his parents after the north tower had been hit. Gordon, who was very close to his family, liked to visit with them whenever his work with Sandler O'Neill & Partners Investments allowed him to travel to Minneapolis. He told his parents that he was fine and that there was nothing to worry about. He said he would call them later that day. His parents never heard from him again.

On the 99th floor, employees working for AON Corporation were in disbelief over the tragedy that had just struck the north tower. Many were in favor of evacuating and going home. Some lingered, trying to decide what to do. But then there had been an announcement, assuring all that everything was safe and secure. They should keep working.

A few minutes later, the second jet struck, the lower portion of the plane slicing through the 70th and adjacent floors of the South Tower.

Dozens of AON employees were never heard from again.

John C. Hartz, 64, and Paul Rizza, 34, were also at work that morning. John was the senior vice president at Fiduciary Trust International, and Paul, an investors services officer. With over 245,156 employess world wide, Fiduciary Trust had offices on the 90th and 94-97 floor, where along with John and Paul, hundreds worked.

They too had heard the explosion, and they too may have thought of leaving work that day, but they stayed. They were dedicated employees. Besides it was the north Tower where the explosion had occurred, and there had been an announcement: "Everything was safe and secure." They went back to work.

John and Paul's loved one's never got to see them again.

David Berry, Christopher Michael Duffy, and David Campbell, were at their desks, and had been working since 8 that morning.

David, the Executive Vice President and Director of Research for Keefe, Bruyette & Woods, a securities broker, was one of the nation's top banking analysts. Keefe, Bruyette & Woods maintained offices on the 85, 88, and 89th floors. The financial news web site, The Street.com, had named Berry "the best stock picker" for banks. After the first jet hit, he had called a number of friends and colleagues to assure them he was safe. There had even been an announcement: "The building is secure. Everything is under control."

Christopher Michael Duffy, was a trader, and David Campbell a senior vice president at Keefe, Bruyette & Woods. They too heard the reassuring announcement.

David Berry, Christopher, and David Campbell were still at work when the second jet hit.

Their families, their loved ones, their children, wives, and parents, never got to see them again.

It was 9:03 a.m.

Brent Woodall was on the 89th floor when the first jetliner crashed into the north tower. He and his wife Tracy, who was five months pregnant, had recently bought a home in Oradell, New Jersey. Their dream home was about 20 miles from his office at the World Trade Center; commuting distance—he wanted to spend as much time as possible with his wife and growing family. Brent was a stock trader for Keefe, Bruyette & Woods. He called his father in southern California to tell him not to worry. He too had heard the reassuring announcement.

"It's no big thing," he assured his father. "It's not my building. I'm safe."

Brent was not easily frightened. He was tough. He was an athlete. He had played tight end at U.C. Berkeley, when Steve Mariucci (current head coach for the San Francisco 49ers) was offensive coordinator. Brent was the kind of guy everyone liked.

He was someone you could count on.

Ten minutes later, Brent made a second call, to his wife, Mary and left a message: "The buildings been hit" he said. Everything was in chaos. He was going to find a way out.

Mary never heard from him again.

Monica Iken received a call from her husband, Michael a few minutes after the plane struck. He told her that he and his colleagues had decided to evacuate his brokerage office in the south tower, which was on the 84th floor. A colleague later remembered that he had last seen Michael on the stairwell near the 60th floor. He had been helping someone down the stairs. Michael was never seen again.

Sonya Perez was working as a clerk typist and had been placed by a temporary agency, and assigned to an office on the 79th floor that morning. It was a new job, it was her first day and it was this day that a jetliner struck the south tower. She was talking to her mother and was still on the phone when the second jet hit. The line went dead.

Kirsten Janssen Santiago was also at work on the 79th floor of the south tower. After the second jet slammed into her building, she called her husband Peter, an Amtrak security guard, and then her aunt, Cheryl Davis, to tell them she was fine. The last thing she said was: "I love you." Then, her line went dead.

"Reuben Perez," 47, along with dozens of other "illegal immigrants," was delivering coffee and sandwhiches that morning, Reuben had worked a lot of "menial" and back breaking jobs, including a brief stint fighting forest fires for the California Conservation Corps—back when he had a "green card."

Delivering food to hungry offices workers was a great job—some of the office employees would often reward him with a handsome tip.

Reuben knew about the explosion in the north Tower—and he worried about some of his friends. He was still worrying, as made his rounds on the 80th floor—and that was when the second jet hit.

"The floor, it exploded. I went up into the air and against a wall. The wall, everything, it fell down on top of me. There was fire. Flames. Smoke. Lots of black smoke. And water. I crawled. It was hot. My back hurt. I couldn't find my shoe. Everything was burning. I could hear screaming. Lots of screaming. I kept crawling. I saw people rushing back and forth. They were screaming. Some were on fire. There was a big hole where the floor was and some fell... down through the hole. But there was smoke, black smoke. They could not see. So much smoke I could not breath. I took my shirt and put it in the water. I wrapped my wet shirt around my face. I crawled to where there was not so much smoke...the floor was hot—my hands and knees were burning... but I found the stairs... the stairs, they were twisted, broken, bent... and there was much smoke. I knew there was fire... I knew there was fire burning down below. I wrapped my shirt tight around my head. I kept going."

Hundreds of people were instantly incinerated when the second jet slammed into the south Tower, between the 70th and 80th floors. Others were instantly dehydrated and overcome by the tremendous heat. They fell by the dozens, like rag dolls, to the floor. Yet others were overcome by the fumes and billowing black smoke, and they too, after staggering around in a blind suffocating panic, toppled to the floor.

Perhaps as many as a thousand people, in the south tower, and another thousand in the north, died within minutes; burnt alive, or overcome by heat and smoke.

Many more died because the raging fires and the massive destruction left them trapped with no escape.

Some, in a blind panic, raced for the phones to scream for help that would never come. Some, realizing the hopelessness of their fate, scribbled last minute notes or tried to call their loved ones to say goodbye. Yet others tried to break out the windows, to obtain breathing air. But the windows held steady, and like the others, these people too had to die.

And then, there were those who stood and climbed out onto

the broken frames of the blown out windows, as fires raced toward them. They screamed and cried for help, gestulating, hoping for salvation from those down below. As the approaching fires raged behind them, they climbed up on top of one another, in order to escape the suffocating fumes and the choking billowing black smoke. But there was no escape, and they began dropping to the ground, a 1000 feet below.

Many of those in adjoining offices and on the floors above and below died because upon witnessing the catastrophic destruction, and in seeing that death was near, they became literally petrified with fear. They sat or lay or stood unmoving, frozen-in-fear, like stone.

And even as the fires raced toward them, many may have remained unmoving, as if already dead. Indeed, it is well known that under conditions of extreme fear, some victims may enter trance-like states, and become so paralyzed and numb with fear that they may appear catatonic, and may fail to make any effort to save their lives.

Some victims become so stiff and rigid, it appears as if rigor mortis has aleady set in—as if they are already dead. They may become so psychologically and emotionally numb that they may even resist and fail to respond to those who are trying to save them.

It is well established that in air and sea disasters 10-25% of the victims may become frozen, stunned, and immobile. Those afflicted will also fail to take any action to save their lives, such as attempting to evacuate a burning or sinking craft even though they have been uninjured. The airline industry has referred to these fear-induced stiffening reactions as "frozen panic states."

Fear-driven catatonic-paralytic states are prevalent in the animal kingdom. These animals are in fact petrified with fear—and this can be very adaptive. Since movement and motion typically alerts a predator to potential prey and thus triggers a savage attack, lack of movement sometimes eliminates the attack. This is also referred to as "death-feigning" or "playing possum."

Hence, by freezing and not-moving, a potential victim may save its life as predators may cease to respond or even fail to note the presence of potential prey.

Many of those in the south and north Towers died because they literally became scared to death and petrified with fear.

Thousands of those who died, however, did so not because they were frightened, but because they experienced insufficient fear.

Mike Wilson, who worked on the 51st floor, reported that many of his co-workers opted to wait in their offices because the stairwells were too crowded.

Others died because they believed the danger had passed, that the fires were contained down below, and so they stayed in their offices and were still there when the towers collapsed.

"People figured that once the plane hit, that was it," Mike later reported. "People didn't think that the buildings were going to fall down."

Others were saved precisely because they were afraid the towers would fall down.

"I was talking with one of my colleagues outside his office on the 62nd floor of the south tower. We were discussing what had happened and what we should do. I wasn't reassured by the announcement. I didn't believe everything was under control. I was in favor of calling it a day and going home. Suddenly the whole building began to sway back and forth and then I heard this tremendous explosion. I thought the whole building was going to topple over and collapse. The ceiling began to buckle and smoke and toxic fumes began pouring into the office. It wasn't just smoke...the ceiling seemed to be dripping fire. We grabbed wet paper towels and put them over our faces. Everyone was running and screaming and just going crazy. I could think of only one thing. I was going to get the hell out of there. I sprinted past the elevator to the stairwell and literally leaped down the stairs. I could think of only one thing: This building is going to collapse and I've got to get out of here."

Brian Clark, a brokerage firm executive, was at work on the 84th floor. He had been working at his desk when the first jetliner pierced the north tower. At first, he and the others thought there had been some terrible accident. The idea of a hijacking, a Kamikaze suicide and a terrorist plot to commit mass murder had not occurred to anyone. Why would it? The idea seemed absurd.

After receiving assurances that it had been nothing more than an accident and that they were not in danger, he and the others went back to work. He heard the same announcement that everything was "under control and secure."

Not everyone was happy at the idea of being forced to stick around—including Brian. Many hesitated and spoke of going home and taking the rest of the day off. Like Brian, many had experienced the 1993 bombing firsthand.

The announcement, however, had been authoritative. "Everything was under control and secure."

Brian went back to work. " I was itching to leave, when, all of a sudden, the building began to rock." The building shook and swayed. Ceiling tiles rained down on his head and now there was smoke and toxic fumes filling the air.

Brian and his coworkers fled for the stairs. Some hesitated before the elevators but Brian and some of the others warned them it would be death trap.

They didn't listen: Said the elevator would be the fastest way down. They were wrong. Many of the elvators were in fact death traps. Most did not work at all.

Brian headed down the stairwell, which was also filling up with smoke. He wondered if there was a fire down below. When he reached the 81st floor, he heard someone crying out for help. Exiting the increasingly smoky stairwells, he followed the cries and discovered and then freed a man buried beneath fallen debris. He helped him to the stairwell "but when we got there everybody had disappeared...all the people I was with. All I could think of was that maybe they went back up because they were afraid there were flames down below."

"I continued down, and by the time I reached the 75th floor, there was water pouring down the stairs. There were fumes and smoke, making it difficult to breath. The stairway was also filling up with people. It was hot. Stuffy, and getting hotter—because of all the sweaty people, because of the fires."

"It was taking longer and longer to get down. We would walk down a few steps and then stop. It reminded me of driving on the freeway in California during rush hour. Cars would be bumper to bumper and then would slow and then just stop. There never seemed to be any reason for it. Now here we were doing the same. Down a few steps and then we would stop. Some of the stops were for three or four minutes. It didn't make any sense."

"A couple of men left the stairwell long enough to break into a vending machine. They began passing out Cokes, Pepsis, and grape sodas.

"Water began pouring down the stairwell. Someone made a joke about how the water from fire hoses and sprinklers was ruining their new shoes."

It took a long time to reach the bottom floor.

"When I finally stepped out into the main floor, and then the street, I saw a police officer who told us to "run...run for it. Now!'"

The sky was falling. It was raining glass and metal. And bodies.

"I began to run but then I stopped and looked back."

"There were people leaping from the flaming towers. People in ties and jackets, free-falling backwards with their hands out."

"It was like a nightmare. I couldn't stand it. People were running now, trying to get away, and I started running with them."

Today, Brian calls himself "a very lucky guy."

A few moments later, the south tower collapsed. It was 10:05 am.

AMERICAN AIRLINES FLIGHT 77

Hani Hajour, Majed Moqed, Nawaq and Salem Alhamzi and Khalid al-Midhar made up the suicide hijacking team that would commandeer American Airlines Flight 77.

They arrived together in a rented car, and and then passed through the boarding gate for American Airlines Flight 77 without drawing any attention. Quietly they took their seats, which were strategically assigned in different areas of the plane.

Hani Hajour was to pilot the aircraft. He took a seat in the first class business section near the cockpit. His assigned target: The Pentagon.

American Airlines Flight 77, a Boeing 757 was now en route from Dulles Airport outside Washington to Los Angeles. There were 58 passengers on board and six crew members including the pilot, Charles Burlingame—whose birthday was the very next day—David Charlebois, copilot, and Jennifer and Kenneth Lewis, who were married and working together as flight attendants.

Zoe, 8, and her sister, Dana 3, were probably squirming with delight. They and their parents, Georgetown University professor Leslie Whittington, and Charles Falkenberg, were headed for Australia, where their mother was to be a visiting fellow at the National University in Canberra. It was going to be an exciting adventure. They thought they were going to live in Australia for a whole year. They would all be dead within an hour.

For Barbara Olson, 45, former federal prosecutor and conservative political commentator, it was supposed to be just another routine flight —one that she wasn't even originally scheduled to be on.

Initially planning to fly out on Monday, Barbara delayed her trip for a day. She wanted to have breakfast with her husband U.S. Solicitor General Theodore Olson, who argues President

Bush's cases before the Supreme Court. She wanted to have a quiet morning celebration of his birthdate, which fell on Tuesday, September 11.

Barbara was intelligent, talented and ambitious. She was a chief investigator for the House Government Reform Committee in the mid-1990s and later worked as a lawyer on the staff for Senate Minority Whip Don Nickles. A frequent critic of the Clinton administration, she wrote a highly unflattering work about Hillary Rodham Clinton, called: Hell to Pay. Sales figures for "Hell to Pay" would rise significantly in the following days.

Like many American women, Barbara carried a cell phone in her purse. Later during the flight, she would twice call her husband to tell him the plane had been hijacked and to ask for instructions.

Initially, Barbara probably didn't pay any attention to the five Middle Eastern men, such as Hani Hajour, who had seated themselves strategically in different areas of the plane. She was busy and had a lot of work to do.

Christopher Newton was also on board. An executive for Work Life Benefits of Cypress, he had recently moved with his wife and children to Arlington, Virginia. He was taking this flight to retrieve his yellow Labrador, who had been left behind with friends in California, until the rest of the family settled into their new home.

Christopher had a good reason for moving to the East Coast. A dedicated dad, Little League Coach and Cub Scout Leader, Christopher deeply loved his wife and children, and was worried that he was not spending enough time with them. When his company relocated from California to Virginia, he spent most of his time commuting on airplanes, traveling some 200,000 miles a year to the East Coast. By moving his family into a new home in Virginia, he hoped to spend more quality time with his wife and their two children, ages 7 and 10.

Those dreams would soon come to an end.

Ruben Ornedo, 39, of Eagle Rock, was not even originally

scheduled for this flight. He was supposed to leave next week. A satellite communications engineer for Boeing, with a computer engineering degree from UCLA, Ruben had been sent to Washington for an extended business trip. But he missed his wife, who was pregnant.

The Ornedos had just bought a house which he had been renovating for the new addition to their family. Given an unexpected two-day lull in his duties, he seized the chance to rush home and see his wife—they had been married only three months.

He would never get to see his wife again.

Paul Ambrose had only been engaged a week. Paul was an exceptional, spectacular guy. His fiance was a lucky girl—and she knew it. Although he was only 32, Paul had already earned his M.D., had gone back to school and earned a masters in public health at Harvard, and was working with the Surgeon General of the United States to help address racial and ethnic disparities in health and health care. Paul had dedicted his entire exceptional but short life to helping people—and now, 5 hijackers were going to end that exceptional life forever.

Rae Sopper, 35, was intending to start a whole new life, one she had been dreaming of for years. A natural athlete with a love of teaching, she had just quit her job as a lawyer in a Washington firm in order to become the new women's gymnastics coach at U.C. Santa Barbara.

Years before, Rae coached gymnastics at the Colorado Gymnastics Institute and at a Junior Olympics Center in Dallas. She also coached at the U.S. Naval Academy, where she served as an attorney with the judge advocate general.

The opportunity to coach again, and for U.C. Santa Barbara, was a chance of a lifetime, the opportunity to pursue her beloved dream. Ten-minutes into her flight, this dream was shattered and would become a nightmare.

Bernard Brown had "style." He had "charisma." And, he was always a very sharp dresser. Bernard Brown was 11 years old. Bernard was smart. He was special, and although he was only 11, he was already thinking of someday becoming a marine biologist, which is why he, and two other school boys, had been picked to go on a 4-day National Geographic Society school trip to the Channel Islands off Santa Barbara. That was why he was on Flight 77. And that was why he and his two 11-year old friends, Asia Cottom and Rodney Dickens, would die.

In the twisted, fevered minds of the hijackers, Bernard Brown, Asia Cottom, Rodney Dickens, and Zoe and Dana 3, like all Americans, like all American children, were enemies of Islam.

Not all those on board with connections to Saudi Arabia and the Middle East were terrorists. Yeneneh Betru, 35, was a native of Ethiopia who had been raised in Saudi Arabia. Years before, he had come to the United States for his education and to pursue his childhood dream of becoming a physician. Yeneneh earned his medical degree at the University of Michigan.

Now that one dream was fulfilled, Yeneneh was on his way towards fulfilling another. Yeneneh had been in Ethiopia. He had fallen in love and was thinking about getting married. Now he was flying back to California to share the happy news with his family.

His family would never hear from him again—the terrorists had decided to end his life, because he and the other Americans were enemies that deserved to be hideously killed.

There was also a retired Rear Admiral on Flight 77, Wilson Flagg. An experienced pilot, he had flown F-8 Crusader supersonic jets in Vietnam and had logged more flying time on that aircraft than any other pilot. He had also flown photo reconnaissance missions after the war.

Always a rising star, Wilson became a rear admiral in 1987. Soon thereafter he was posted at the Pentagon as one of the top officers for the Naval Reserve. In this capacity, he organized the 1991 Tailhook Conference, named after the device that catches planes landing on an aircraft carrier. "Tailhook" however, meant much more than that. The term had a double meaning: The hooking of tail. These events were notoriously wild affairs, with lots of drinking and sex.

The 1991 Conference spawned the infamous Tailhook sexual harassment scandal and Wilson Flagg took the fall and retired.

Wilson and his wife, Darlene Flagg, boarded Flight 77 together, and were returning home after attending the 40th reunion of his academy class in Annapolis. Wilson and Darlene were high school sweethearts. They were married after Wilson graduated from the U.S. Naval Academy. Still deeply in love, the couple split their time between a home in Las Vegas and a cattle ranch in Virginia. Holding hands, they settled in for the long flight home.

For Wilson and Darlene Flagg, as well as for countless others, this trip would be anything but routine. Soon after takeoff, Flight 77 was hijacked. It would crash into the Pentagon at 9:40 a.m., killing all aboard.

******

At first, the flight continued along its designated route without incident. The jet flew as far as the Ohio-Kentucky border. Then, the terrorists made their move.

It was a chilling and well choreographed operation. Again flight attendants were threatened and attacked. The pilots were overpowered. The flight attendants and all of the passengers were herded to the back of the jet —as far away from the cockpit as possible.

Unbeknownst to the passengers, the pilots, having been tied up, were now being stabbed to death and killed.

Air traffic controllers quickly realized something was amiss when the plane deviated from its usual flight path to Los Angeles. It changed directions and turned east.

It roared at full speed, directly toward Washington.

Air traffic controllers became even more alarmed when they realized someone in the cockpit had turned off the jet's transponder. The transponder transmits information about an airplane's identification, direction of flight, speed and altitude.

Flight 77 had completely disappeared from the radar screen.

Later, controllers spotted an unidentified aircraft moving at an unusually high speed toward the White House.

Alarm turned to panic when controllers received word about the two jets that had crashed into the World Trade Center. Suddenly what was occurring began to make sense. It was a chilling, horrifying realization.

Controllers immediately telephoned air traffic control at Ronald Reagan Washington National Airport near the Pentagon and then the White House to warn of another terrorist attack.

Barbara Olson reached for her cell phone and called her husband, Solicitor General Theodore Olson.

"Can you believe this...we are being hijacked," she said. There are at least two hijackers on board, she said, and they were armed with knives and a cardboard cutting knife. Then the line went dead.

Ted Olson immediately contacted authorities at the Justice Department to advise them of the situation. Then, his phone rang again. It was Barbara.

Ted Olson told his wife about the two jets that had struck the World Trade Center in New York. She and the flight crew should know that they were in great danger.

"What should I tell the pilot to do?" she asked. Barbara was used to taking charge.

Suddenly, the jet pivoted in a tight circle and looped west toward the Pentagon. It vanished from controllers' screens as it rapidly descended and dropped below the radar.

It was 9:40 a.m.

9:43 A.M. THE WHITE HOUSE & PENTAGON

9:43 am: American Airlines Flight 77, a Boeing 757 enroute from Dulles Airport outside Washington to Los Angles with 58 passengers and six crew members, crashes into the Pentagon. One of the building's five sides collapses.

9:45 am: The White House is evacuated

******

At 9:40 a.m., President Bush was in Florida. He was speaking at the Emma E. Booker Elementary School in Sarasota.

Vice President Cheney, was ensconced in the White House. He was watching television, engrossed in the details of this catastrophe, which had struck the financial heart of the nation.

According to the Vice President, he had been watching television coverage of the first crash when the second plane struck.

"Immediately that triggered in my mind, the thought of terrorism." He called President Bush.

A few minutes later, Bush made a statement, describing the attacks on the World Trade Center as acts of apparent terrorism.

Cheney was next informed that his life may be in danger. Vice President Cheney made a dash for safety.

When aides entered the room where he was still watching TV, they told him that a Boeing 757, an American Airlines commercial jet had been hijacked by terrorists. They feared that it might be headed directly toward the White House.

Cheney later reported he had been told the jet entered the "danger zone," which is why he sought safety.

"Sir, we have to leave immediately," agents told the Vice President. At full gallop Cheney was escorted and evacuated to the White House basement. His safety assured he reached for a secure telephone and contacted President Bush.

Bush was urged, in no uncertain terms, "to delay his return" to Washington.

"I said, 'Delay your return. We don't know what's going on here, but it looks like we've been targeted.'"

Bush and his entourage sped off to the Sarasota-Bradenton airport, and from there it was to Barksdale Air Force Base in Louisiana, where Bush was surrounded by Air Force personnel with M-16s at the ready.

The Commander in Chief, the leader of the free world, still did not feel safe. There was a concern that the terrorists may even have access to a nuclear device. Only an underground command bunker that could withstand a direct hit by an atomic bomb would suffice. He was whisked away to Nebraska's Offutt Air Force Base and ground zero of the U.S. Strategic Command.

Bush remained in an atomic bomb-proof bunker until assured that his life was no longer at risk.

The President and Vice President of the United States were conviced they were being targeted by terrorists. The two men believed that the White House, home to the President of the United States and symbol of our nation and democracy was the target of terrorists interested in its total destruction.

But striking the White House turned out to be a more difficult task than the hijackers anticipated—if in fact it was their target at all. It was tougher to see than the hijackers may have been led to believe.

They were coming in low from the west and the Old Executive Office Building hindered their view of President Bush's home.

Blindsided by the huge old building and lacking adequate visual aides, American Airlines Flight 77 turned away, circled round and headed toward the Pentagon—which, as based on radar images, may well have been its target all along.

Many of those at work at the Pentagon that morning, were watching TV in disbelief, mesmerized by the horrific, hellish images of the World Trade Center's demise.

Others were talking on the phones to colleagues, wives and relatives about the disaster, assuring loved ones that the Pentagon was the "safest, most fortified building on the planet."

Army Lt. Col. Jerry Kitzhaber was busy at his desk when his wife called to tell him about what had occurred in New York City.

"Are you okay?" she asked.

He laughed and reassured her. "This is the Pentagon. I should be okay here."

And then....

Boom!!

Commander Robert Edeward Dolan was in the Navy-wing that morning. He was one of the Navy's rising stars. At the tender age of 40, he had become commander of the USS John Hancock, whose motto was: "First for Freedom."

Although a Navy-man through and through, Commander Dolan preferred to spend his off duty hours with family. On weekends and evenings, he coached his son Beau's Little League baseball team.

Commander Dolan had just been transferred into the newly renovated offices of the D Ring's first floor.

At 9:43 a.m., the D Ring was completely pulverized by Flight 77.

A lot of men and women were working in D ring that day.

Lt. Commander David Williams, 32, had been on the phone when the jet struck. He had been talking to his wife, discussing the World Trade Center tragedy, when, the line went dead.

There was a horrific explosion as the aircraft, flying fast and low barreled into the Pentagon and ripped through the newly renovated walls of the "world's most secure office building."

"We heard a huge blast and then the whole building shook,"

said Terry Yonkers, an Air Force civilian employee. "There was screaming and pandemonium."

The jet had plowed a crater 100 feet wide that ripped away the walls of all five stories of the building, collapsing the outermost rings, which encircle the Pentagon.

The nerve center of the world's preeminent military and the symbol of America's unassailable military might had been penetrated, cracked and split open like a broken egg.

Secondary explosions followed the first nightmarish blast. Black smoke and flames began billowing from the ruined sections of the building. A Klaxon horn began screaming to alert workers to danger.

A hurried but calm exodus of civilian and military personnel ensued. Among them was Secretary of Defense, Donald Rumsfeld who immediately began assisting victims of the attack.

Others stood at windows in the inner ring, watching in shock and disbelief as firefighters struggled against the blazes that raged.

The Pentagon had suddenly become the middle of a war zone. Many of the personnel on duty that day felt as if they were living through a modern day Pearl Harbor.

20,000 uniformed and civilian workers had been working on September 11 in the cavernous headquarters of the U.S. armed forces. They were doing their jobs—attending to the security of the nation and the world. Now, the symbol of the world's mightiest military power lay crippled, naked and exposed. The jet had smashed a huge gaping hole across all five floors, killing and maiming hundreds of men and women.

Much of the damage had been inflicted on the Navy-wing of the Pentagon. The fires burned so ferociously, it was so incredibly hot, that it was nearly an hour before rescue workers could even approach the rubble to begin searching for suvivors.

As the conflagration raged, emergency workers began digging a trench in order to separate the bombed-out Navy wing of the building from the adjacent Army offices. This cut the building in two, in order to isolate the still-burning fires and keep them from spreading to other offices of the nation's military headquarters.

For the next two hours, fire officials desperately fought the blazes as rescuers made a frantic search for survivors. It was a tough and stubborn fight. The solid construction and fortifications of the World War II-era building were making the fires extremely difficult and hazardous to combat. Here and there, fuel from the ruined jet was also igniting. Specialized equipment needed to be brought in.

American Flight 77 crashed into the Pentagon at 9:43 am. As late as 11:30 am, firefighters were still spraying water on the burning remains. The fires would not be contained until noon. They would continue to burn into the next day.

Workers attacked the building, searching for survivors, and using heavy cranes and other equipment to keep the burning offices separated from the Army wing to the north. The Federal Emergency Management Agency (FEMA) sent out four teams to assist in the rescue effort.

Kenneth Foster, soon joined in the effort to rescue those buried in the steaming rubble. He was on the scene within minutes after the jet hit. He kept a 44 hour vigil and did not leave until he had been told to go home and get some rest. But he couldn't rest. He and his wife, Sandra Foster, were supposed to attend a training session that afternoon for prospective parents. They were planning to adopt a baby girl.

Hired right out of high school, Sandra Foster had worked for the Pentagon for 25 years, and was looking forward to being a new mom. When the plane hit, Sandra was killed instantly.

"Everyone should have a wife like Sandra," Kenneth later said. "She was an angel. An absolute angel."

Carolyn Halmon was also among "the missing." She had arrived early that morning, courtesy of her husband, Herman, who also worked at the Pentagon but in the evenings. He had volunteered to bring her to work that day, because as he explained later, he loved her so and wanted to squeeze in as many kisses as possible before she went into work. When he got back home, he heard about the crash and frantically called her office over and over again.

She would never answer her phone again.

Lt. General Timothy J. Maude, 54, was the highest-ranking military officer killed that day. It was General Maude who was largely responsible for the Army's highly successful new recruiting slogan, "An Army of One."

General Maude was "An Army of One" a very brave highly decorated soldier who had served in Viet Nam. He had been awarded the Legion of Merit, the Bronze Star and a Defense Superior Service award. He had died, while trying to rescue others.

A lot of good men and women lost their lives that day, including Johnnie Doctor, Jr., 32, a Navy man and Information Systems Technician, and Commanders William Howard Donovan, Jr. 37, Patrick Dunn, 39, and Scott Powell.

Scott Powell's identical twin brother, Art, also worked at the Pentagon.

Scott and Art Powell were not married to the military but to life. At one time they called themselves the "Mable's Twinzz" and had formed a music production company, "Dem Twinzz productions." They had been classically trained in music and together played keyboard, acoustic guitar and bass. They would incorporate thousands of musical sounds into their own music. Ironically, both developed a passion for Arabic song, which they played while on a tour together in Sweden and the United Kingdom.

The duo would never perform together again. Over the ensuing days and weeks after the Pentagon catastrophe, friends and family, so long accustomed to being around the two brothers, called Art, because the two twins sounded alike, and they missed the sound of Scott's voice.

Army Lt. Col. Kenny Cox, who fought through black smoke to rescue survivors, said, "This is a cheap, dirty, senseless way to attack somebody."

Dogs trained in differentiating bodies and live victims were airlifted to the scene. Rescuers were also employing sophisticated miniature cameras that could be snaked between the rubble as well as acoustical listening devices that could pick up the faintest sound.

Yet, no survivors were found.

A Defense Department statement was issued later that day, which said no one could have survived the impact and the resulting fire.

The consequences were catastrophic.

Upon surveying the damage, one service woman said: "If the Pentagon isn't secure, maybe none of us are."

Two hours later, several flatbed trucks carrying almost a hundred metal coffins were parked outside the Pentagon.

Hundreds were dead and injured. Though some newspapers speculated that there would be over 800 victims, Pentagon spokeswoman Victoria Clarke dismissed a reported estimate of at least 800 dead. "We do not as yet have casualty figures," she explained. "I have no confidence in the 800 number. I have no confidence in any number."

Later that day, it was determined that 50 Army and 50 Navy personnel were missing, including Major Wallace Hogan, Jr., who had served with the Green Berets and the Special Forces. Major Hogan had recently been promoted, becoming a General's aide, which is why he was at the Pentagon that morning.

A "gung ho" Army man, Hogan often said he would serve until they kicked him out. His only concern about working in the military was his recent promotion. He was pleased at the honor, but worried that the extra hours he would be working as a General's aide, would take him away from his wife.

He loved his wife.

He would never see his wife again.

Angela Houtz, 27, was also unaccounted for. Angela was brilliant. Her instructors remembered her as having one of the best minds they had ever encountered.

She was smart, she was classy, she was the class salutatorian and her picture still hangs on the school's wall of fame.

Everybody liked and respected Angela. When she said something, people listened.

On the evening of September 11, people were still listening, hoping for some sound, some sign, that Angela had somehow survived.

Peggy Hurt, 36, was also among the missing. She had only worked at the Pentagon for two weeks. And then there was Judith Jones, Lt. Col. Dennis Johnson, Major Steve Long, Lt. Michael Scott Lamana, David Laychak, Robert Hymel, Terrance Lynch and Brenda Kegler who was so afraid of airplanes falling from the sky that she refused to fly.

All these individuals, who worked in the "world's most secure office building" were dead.

The total dead would not be known for days.

Including those who perished on board Flight 77, the final numbers were estimated at 189 missing and presumed dead.

If it had not been for the ongoing renovation, the number of dead would have been catastrophic. For the loved ones of those unaccounted for, each death was a personal catastrophe.

It was a catastrophe!

The number of civilian casualties and injuries was extensive.

There were some workers who managed to escape, though they were severely injured and horribly burned. David King, Juan Santiago Cruz, Antoinette Sherman, Raquel Kelly, Latisha Hook, Brian Birdwell, Kevin Shaeffer and Louise Kurtz had all been badly burned. Almost a hundred more had been severely injured and taken to local hospitals.

"The fire was intense," Rear Adm. Craig Quigley, the Pentagon spokesman, told reporters.

Dennis Wang, a doctor at a Washington D.C. hospital described the severity of the injuries. He reported that over 100 feet of human skin would be needed just to help dress the severe burns of just eight unfortunate souls. He further warned that even if they survived the next 24 hours, they were at a high risk of infection, organ failure, shock and death.

Some consider that the pain and suffering resulting from severe burning is a fate worse than death.

Louise Kurtz, 49, of Stafford County had started work as an Army accountant at the Pentagon only two days before. She had been working near the Navy-wing when the jet slammed into the structure. The burning jet fuel quickly snaked from building to building setting adjacent offices on fire, including the offices were she had just started to work.

Washington Hospital Center officials described her as in critical condition, with severe burns over 70 percent of her body.

Louise was so badly burned, that her husband, Michael Kurtz was unable to recognize her: "I didn't recognize my wife of 31 years... I saw a person who looked like a mummy."

She was in and out of consciousness. According to Kurtz, at first she was almost completely unresponsive, with one exception: she moved her head when he told her he loved her.

******

Back at the Pentagon, crews continued to desperately search for survivors and to put out the last of the fires. Suddenly, military helicopters began buzzing overhead. An alarm sounded.

"Another commercial jetliner has been spotted," officials yelled. "It's only 20 miles away and headed right for us."

"Three bogeys are headed towards us. Move!" a white coated woman yelled.

Emergency and construction workers, police, civilians, military personnel and construction workers started fleeing for safety, trying to put as much ground between them and the Pentagon as possible.

"Where are our fighter planes to shoot it down?" people shouted.

With fear and trembling, they hunkered down in safety, waiting waiting for the hijacked jet to appear and wondering why airforce jets had not yet taken to the air, to shoot it down.

They waited. They watched.

It was a false alarm.

Or was it?

******

It was 10:00 am

The President of the United States had reason to believe that there were perhaps as many as six commercial jets which had been hijacked by Kamikaze-style terrorists.

The choice was clear. There was only one viable option.

President Bush issued an executive order. The military was to shoot down hijacked commercial airliners if necessary, to protect the citizens of the United States.

"I gave our military the orders necessary to protect Americans, do whatever it would take to protect Americans," Bush said later. "And of course that's difficult."

As detailed by Vice President Cheney, "We knew there was at least one, perhaps several more hijacked planes in the air. They had to be intercepted. If the plane would not divert, or if they wouldn't pay any attention to instructions to move away from the city, as a last resort our pilots were authorized to take them out."

"Now people say," Cheney continued, "that that's a horrendous decision to make. Well, it is. You've got an airplane full of American citizens, civilians, captured by terrorists and you are going to, in fact, shoot it down and kill all those Americans on board. But you have to ask yourself: If we had had combat air patrol up over New York, and we'd had the opportunity to take out the two aircraft that hit the World Trade Center, would we have been justified in it? And I think absolutely we would have."

In fact, jet fighters were scrambled to take out and destroy the airliners that would eventually destroy the Twin Towers of the World Trade Center. At 8:44 am Tuesday, after it became clear that American Airlines Flight 11 from Boston to Los Angeles had been hijacked and had turned south toward New York City, two F-15 jet fighters were scrambled from Otis Air Force Base on Cape Cod, Massachusetts. But they were unable to intercept the doomed aircraft in time.

Two more F-16s had been scrambled from Langley Air Force Base at 9:42 am but had been in the air for only two minutes when American Flight 77 crashed into the Pentagon.

Now the President of the United States had reason to suspect that there could be three more planes with terrorists at the controls. Jet fighters were being scrambled.

There was in fact one more hijacked airline still in the air.

United Airlines Flight 93, originally bound from Newark, NJ to San Francisco, California was at that very moment on its way toward Washington. Its destination, the White House—home to the President of the United States.

******

UNITED AIRLINES FLIGHT 93

United Airlines Flight 93 was supposed to be the first of the four hijacked jets to leave the ground. The other three flights would depart shortly thereafter. Each hijacked jet had its own unique target.

The terrorist's plan called for coordinated attacks which were to occur within minutes of each other. By having the assaults timed so closely together, government authorities would be prevented from effectively intervening. There would be insufficient time to evacuate targeted buildings, such as the White House, Pentagon, or the World Trade center, thus increasing the number of casualties, which the hijackers probably hoped might even include the killing of the President of the United States.

Instead, the departure of Flight 93 was delayed. It was the last to be hijacked and the last to crash into the ground.

******

Jason Dahl, 43, was the pilot of United Airlines Flight 93. Jason lived in Littleton, Colorado with wife Sandy and his son Matthew, 15. The previous day, he tried to find a pilot to take his place on the doomed flight so that he could spend time with his family.

As they prepared for takeoff, Jason checked the instrument panel and went over the checklist with his copilot, Leroy Homer, 36.

The flight attendants, Sandy Bradshaw, CeeCee Lyles, and the others, were also attending to what was little more than routine, carefully going through the preflight instructions.

Most of the passengers, being seasoned veterans of innumerable flights, paid the flight attendants little attention. There were four notable exceptions: Ziad Jarrahi, Saeed Alghamdi,

Ahmed Alhaznawi and Ahmed Alnami.

Something was wrong.

For some reason, the flight was being delayed.

The jet sat on the ground.

Something was wrong.

The minutes ticked by.

Ten minutes.

Fifteen minutes.

Twenty minutes.

Thirty minutes.

And still, the jet sat on the ground.

It must have seemed an interminable delay to the four hijackers. They were likely becoming increasingly nervous, sweating, twitching in their seats, casting weary glances at one another, wondering if they had been found out and if the FBI was on the way. One or more of the flight attendants may have even noticed their increasing anxiety, and may have tried to reasure them that everything would be OK.

After a 40-minute delay, United Airlines Flight 93, enroute from New Jersey and bound for San Francisco, began its journey down the runway. It took off from Gate 17, Concourse A and flew west, climbing to 35,000 feet.

Flight attendant CeeCee Lyles loved meeting new people and traveling to new places, and today would be no different from any other day, or so she thought. To her, she had the most exciting job in the world.

Cee Cee, Sandy Bradshaw, and the others, began preparing to roll out breakfast.

There would be no bumping of legs with the food cart on this flight.

Although Flight 93 had over 180 seats, the big jet was less than one quarter full. The passengers spread themselves out for more comfort and leg room.

Thomas E. Burnett Jr., 38, a 6-foot-2, former high school quarterback, was a Senior Vice President and CEO of Thoratec.

He was not even supposed to be on this flight. On a whim, he had decided to fly home early because he missed his wife and three daughters, a 3-year-old and 5-year-old twins.

Jeremy Glick, 31, a 6-foot-4, 220 pound former high school wrestler and college judo champ, was returning to California where he worked as a sales manager for a California Internet company. He settled into his seat and began attending to business.

Mark Bingham of San Francisco was the owner of a public relations firm, The Bingham Group, with offices in New York and San Francisco. In addition to running his own business, Mark, 31, was a 6-foot-5 rugby player who had ventured to run with the bulls in Pamplona, Spain, just this summer.

Mark was not a man to mess with. He formerly played on three national championship rugby teams at the University of California at Berkeley and had once wrestled a gun away from a mugger.

Mark had originally planned to fly to San Francisco the day before, but decided to wait until Tuesday to recover from a friend's birthday celebration party. When he overslept, his friend, Matt Hall, rushed him to Newark in time for his plane. Mark was the last to board. He later called Matt to thank him. "Take care, I'll talk to you soon," Mark said.

He was sitting in seat 4D in the rear of the first class section. He would later call his mother to report the plane had been hijacked.

Alan A. Beaven, 48, was a father of three and a San Francisco attorney who specialized in environmental law. Alan was committed to protecting our water and fought against those polluting rivers and streams. A very spiritually minded man, with a deep and profound love for the environment, he had decided to take a year's sabbatical from his law practice to volunteer as the general counsel with Siddha Yoga Meditation in India.

Alan had been working on a Clean Water Act lawsuit filed by fishermen, over the pollution in the American River. He was on his way back to San Francisco to work on this final case. He had just completed a meeting at the Siddha Foundation's U.S. headquarters in South Fallsburg, New York.

Richard Guadagno, 38, was also a lover of wildlife and the environment. He worked as a biologist managing the Humboldt Bay National Wildlife Refuge in Northern California. Richard was a tough guy—a real outdoorsman who lived and enjoyed wildlife.

Richard was on his way home after visiting his parents and was looking forward to returning to California. Richard was soon to be married to Diqui LaPenta, 36, an assistant professor of microbiology at the College of the Redwoods in Eureka. He was about to embark on a whole new chapter in his life—it was to be the last chapter of his life.

There were more women than men on board, including Nicole Miller, Christine Synder, Kriston Gould, Marion Britton, Georgino Corrigan, Linda Gronland, Laruen Grandcolas, Colleen Fraser, Joan Peterson who was traveling with her husband Donald, and Deora Bodley.

Deora Bodley, was starting her junior year at Santa Clara University. She had worked as a teacher's aid and volunteered for organizations like the Special Olympics. Deora was studying to become a psychologist. She wanted to help people. Although Deora first planned on taking another flight, she wanted to leave earlier to get home to her boyfriend and family. She had already missed her original flight, which was scheduled to depart the day before the September 11 attacks.

Nicole Carole Miller, 21, was also a college student from the Santa Clara - San Jose area. Nicole was smart and beautiful, she was on the Dean's List. She had been visting New York with her boyfriend, but when it was time to fly home, she was bumped from his flight. After hugging and kissing at the gate, they each boarded their seperate flights. They would never kiss or hold each other again.

Christine Snyder, 32, of Kailua, Hawaii, was an arborist

working in a forestry. Christine was a newlywed. She had been married only three months. She was anxious to get back home and into the arms of her husband. They would never hold and kiss each other again.

Lauren Grandcolas, 38, was returning from her grandmother's funeral in New Jersey. Minutes into the flight, she would use her cell phone to call her husband: "We have been hijacked," she told him. "I love you."

All these women, all these innocent, talented people, with stars in their eyes and a bright future ahead, with husbands and wives, children, and parents, with boyfriends who loved them—they would all die and would never hold or kiss their loved ones again.

In the fevered, twisted minds of the hijackers, they were Americans and they were enemies of Islam.

The five flight attendants, including Lorraine Bay, Sandra Bradshaw, Wanda Green, and CeeCee Lyles, began serving breakfast.

CeeCee didn't live in San Francisco, though she sometimes stayed overnight depending on her flight schedule. Nor did she live in New Jersey. Her home was Florida, where she lived with her husband, a police officer and four sons.

There were several other passengers with Florida connections. Four of them planned to hijack the plane. Saeed Alghamdi, Ahmed Alhaznawi and Ahmed Alnami were at that very moment preparing to take CeeCee and the other crew members hostage. Ziad Jarrahi was to take the controls and pilot the hijacked plane.

Unbeknownst to any of the passengers, these four Arabic men were bound together in a suicide plot with a mission. They wanted to turn United Airlines Flight 93 into a ticking bomb, crashing it into the White House the home of the President of the United States.

It was time.

Ziad Jarrahi gave the signal and then he and Saeed Alghamdi, Ahmed Alhaznawi and Ahmed Alnami began acting out the drama that would enable them to incapacitate the crew and hijack the plane.

They had rehearsed their movements a hundred times. This well choreographed routine came naturally. First they put on their red head bands. Then came the red box, which they would claim contained a bomb.

They stood up. They acted as one.

Brandishing the ceramic knives they had smuggled past metal detectors, as well as box cutters and razors, several of his men began threatening the flight attendants. His men screamed that this was a hijacking and that they had bombs.

At that moment, a male passenger had just exited the bathroom. He quickly stepped back inside. Using his cell phone, the man called an emergency dispatcher: "We are being hijacked, we are being hijacked! This is not a hoax!"

The terrorists began threatening the passengers, demanding they get up from their seats and move to the back of the plane. One of the men slashed and then killed a passenger to emphasize that they meant business.

The pilots, including Jason Dahl, had been explicitly trained to always cooperate with hijackers. Yet despite their instructions, they resisted and fought at first.

An open mike caught some portions of the cockpit encounter. One of the pilots began to shout: "Get out of here!"

As air traffic controllers listened, the microphone went on and off, over and over again. They heard fighting. Scuffling. One of the pilots yelled again: "Get out of here!"

Again, the microphone started going on and off. And then, an Arabic-accented voice said in broken English: "There is a bomb on board. This is the captain speaking. Remain in your seat. There is a bomb on board. Stay quiet. We are meeting with their demands. We are returning to the airport."

The microphone was then turned off a final time.

The flight attendants and the passengers were being herded by three of the hijackers into the rear of the plane. The hijackers had already killed the pilots.

Ziad Jarrahi sat in the pilot's seat and took control. A second terrorist sat beside him. They locked themselves in the cockpit.

The hijackers then sought to reassure the passengers. As reported by Jeremy Glick, to his wife back in New York:

"They said they were just making a political statement, and if everyone remained calm, they would all get back on the ground safely."

The passengers believed them.

Everything, so far, was going according to plan.

As United Airlines Flight 93 neared Cleveland, it made a U-turn and headed toward Washington. The Cleveland control tower was observing the jet on radar and controllers were surprised when the plane made a sharp 180-degree turn and went to a low altitude.

Ziad Jarrahi was having some trouble controlling the craft. A witness on the ground called 911 to report a large aircraft flying low and banking from side to side.

Many of the passengers were frightened. Others were mad.

Although airborne, modern day airline passengers are by no means cut off from the world. With the wizardry of modern day wireless technology, phone calls can be made and received from anywhere in the world, including United Airlines Flight 93.

The cell phones were humming.

Those with cell phones began calling friends and loved ones to tell them about the hijacking and to say their final good byes and to profess their love.

It was during these calls that some of the passengers learned of the disasters that had befallen the twin towers. Other flights had been hijacked.

Some of the passengers began to fear that this too is what the hijackers had in store.

A few of the men began to whisper among themselves. Thomas Burnett, Mark Bingham, Jeremy Glick, Todd Beamer, were take charge kindof guys, and they began discussing their options.

From the cell-phone calls passengers made and the conversations in the cockpit, federal authorities soon learned the intended target of the suicide pilots was the White House.

Flight attendant CeeCee Lyles called her husband and four sons in Fort Myers, Florida. It was important to her that she talk to them and let them know how much she loved them. In the background, her husband could hear screaming.

Lauren Grandcolas, 36, called her husband, Jack, but he did not answer. So she left a message saying there was trouble on the plane and that there had been a hijacking, but that she was not hurt and was comfortable. She just wanted him to know, she said, that she loved him and their children, very much.

Andrew Garcia, 62, of Portola Valley, California also tried to call his family. But he only got a chance to say one word: "Dorothy," his wife's name. Then the line went dead.

Mark Bingham called his wife, Kathy, from the cabin, ringing his home in Saratoga, at 6:35 am California time. The line went dead. He called back. "Hi Kathy. It's Mark. I just wanted to tell you that I love you and that I love all of you in case I never see you again...I'm on a plane that's being hijacked," he said.

Kathy had been making breakfast and was at first groggy, half asleep. Now she was shocked and scared. She turned on a light and searched for something to write on. She bumped into his mother, Alice Hoglan, who had also come to answer the phone. Alice got on the line.

"Mom," he began, inexplicably becoming formal, "this is Mark Bingham. I just wanted you to know I love you. I'm on United Flight 93 — we have been taken over by hijackers, by three guys who say they have a bomb."

Jeremy Glick called his wife, Lyzbeth from a seat phone. He placed the call to his in-laws' home in upstate New York, where his wife was staying with the couple's 11-week-old daughter, Emerson.

Jeremy began recounting the horror that was unfolding. He told her three knife-wielding Arabs, wearing red headbands had hijacked the plane. They were brandishing a box that they said contained a bomb.

Lyzbeth gasped. "Oh my God, Jeremy's on one of the planes."

"Calm down, you have to be brave, you have to be strong," Jeremy told her.

Lyzbeth's mother used her own cell phone and called 911. State troopers asked questions that were relayed to Jeremy, which he tried to answer.

But then, Jeremy had his own questions:

"How did these people ever get on this flight with knives and bombs? How could this happen?" Jeremy asked. "How could this be, that we could be taken by surprise by these armed people?"

He told his wife that he and the other men were trying to decide what to do. "We're just deciding whether we should do this, are we better off not attacking them?"

The trooper then confirmed what Jeremy had already heard from some of the other passengers. Two other hijacked planes had just hit the World Trade Center.

Glick wanted to know if the other planes were commercial airliners. The answer was yes.

At that point, Glick knew he was riding on a flying bomb that would be used to kill many more than those aboard.

Then, they talked about what Glick planned to do next.

Glick shut off the phone and conferred with some of the other men. A few minutes later, he called his wife back and told her that he and some of the other men were going to try to overpower the hijackers.

"If we are going to crash into something . . . let's not let that happen...Our best chance is to fight these people, rather than accept it." He then added: "I just want you to know how much I love you and the baby."

Thomas Burnett was also talking with Deena, his wife, and told her the plane had been hijacked. "They've already knifed a guy. They're saying they have a bomb."

Thomas Burnett called her two more times to discuss the

situation and then he made one final call: "I know we're all going to die - there's three of us who are going to do something
about it."

Deena was frantic. She pleaded with him not to risk his life,
fearing they would kill him. A former flight attendant, she remembered her training. "I told him to please sit down and not
draw attention to himself."

But Burnett wouldn't hear of it. They were going to get
these guys. Then, he said to his wife, "I love you, honey."

"He told me over and over how much he loved me. He must
have said 'I love you' about a thousand times."

Finally, he told her, "We've decided. We're going to do it."
He told her he would leave the phone off the hook.

Deena gave the phone to her father. She did not want to
hear the rest.

Her father listened:

"It was quiet for a couple of minutes, followed by a series of
screams in the background. Two minutes more of silence came,
followed by more screams, commotion and then more
silence....We were hoping that Jeremy or somebody will come
back and say it worked, or something...but after the screams faded
away there was only a noise that sounded like air passing, maybe
static — it was a non-human noise . . . then it was no noise, it
was silence. We held onto the phone for a couple of hours, but no
one came back on the line."

Todd Beamer, 32, a former high school baseball and basket-
ball star, was an Oracle Executive from New Jersey and the father of two young children. Todd was a religious man who was
very involved in his church. Using an air-phone, he tried to call
his wife, who was five months pregnant with their third child.
He was unsuccessful.

Todd managed to get through to a GTE supervisor, Lisa
Jefferson. She could hear the screaming and commotion in the
background. Todd told her the hijackers had stabbed and may
have killed the pilots and another passenger.

"I am not sure if they are dead or alive," he said. "I also know," he continued, "that we are not going to make it out of here." He then told her, that he, Glick and the others were going to "jump the hijacker with the bomb," the one that was guarding them in the rear of the plane.

Then, he asked Lisa to call his wife and tell her how much he loved her. She promised.

"Thank you," he said, then he recited Psalm 23, the Lord's Prayer:

"The LORD is my shepherd; I shall not want."

"He maketh me to lie down in green pastures: he leadeth me beside the still waters."

"He restoreth my soul: he leadeth me in the paths of righteousness for his name's sake."

"Yea, though I walk through the valley of the shadow of death, I will fear no evil: for thou art with me; thy rod and thy staff they comfort me."

"Thou preparest a table before me in the presence of mine enemies: thou anointest my head with oil; my cup runneth over."

"Surely, goodness and mercy shall follow me all the days of my life: and I will dwell in the house of the LORD for ever."

Todd's were the last words heard by listeners outside the plane:

"God help me. Jesus help me," he said, as Lisa Jefferson listened.

"Are you guys ready?" he shouted!

"Let's roll!"

He dropped the phone.

There were screams and shouts; and then, there was silence.

The jet was now 80 miles southeast of Pittsburgh, soaring over rural Pennsylvania.

They were strangers to one another, Jeremy Glick, Tom Burnett, Todd Beamer and Mark Bingham: successful, take-charge guys, on an early morning cross-country flight. And now fate had brought them together. And now they would die together.

But not without a fight.

All the other men on board agreed to join them in this fight to the finish. They would attack, disarm and then kill the four hijackers and if god be willing, take control of Flight 93 before it crashed.

They advanced toward their red-head-banded opponents: Saeed Alghamdi, Ahmed Alhaznawi, Ahmed Alnami and last of all Ziad Jarrahi as he cowered in the cockpit.

Jeremy Glick, Tom Burnett, Todd Beamer and Mark Bingham, and the others had made a decision to fight. They were not afraid. They were not going to be intimidated.

They were Americans.

They attacked and became entangled in a life and death struggle with the hijackers. Several of the men must have been slashed and stabbed but the desperate struggle continued. Listeners on cell phones heard screaming, scuffling, more screams, and finally silence.

In the cockpit, Ziad Jarrahi could hear the fighting and he knew his unholy cause was lost.

Jeremy Glick, Tom Burnett, Todd Beamer and Mark Bingham, were coming for him.

Jarrahi and his men had failed.

At precisely 10:10 am, Flight 93 plowed into the soft earth of a former strip mine, near Stony Creek Township, in rural southwestern Pennsylvania, killing everyone aboard.

The Attack & Collapse

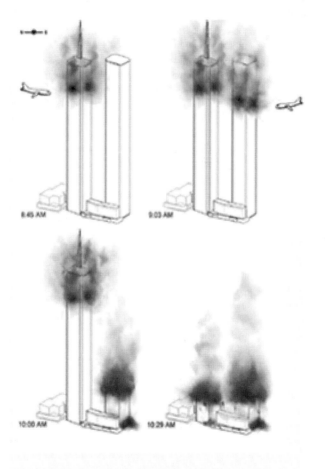

Graphics by Simon Leung and Cindy Ma

THE VALLEY OF THE SHADOW OF DEATH

******

8:45 am: American Airlines Flight 11, a Boeing 767 en route from Boston's Logan Airport to Los Angeles International with 92 people onboard, slams into the north tower of the World Trade Center.

9:03 am: Approximately 18 minutes later, United Airlines Flight 175, a Boeing 767 enroute from Boston to Los Angeles with 65 people onboard, hits the south tower of the World Trade Center.

10:05 am: The south tower of the World Trade Center collapses in a plume of ash and debris.

10:28 am: The World Trade Center's north tower collapses.

5:25 pm: Seven World Trade Center, a 47-story tower, collapses from ancillary damage.

******

Danny Amos: "I was walking along Liberty street, admiring all the buildings and squinting up at the World Trade Center when I saw this jet. It seemed to be flying awfully low. I thought it must be an optical illusion. Maybe it was a lot further away, because otherwise, it was going to hit the north tower. And then, I heard this whoosh. And for a moment, it was as if everything went silent. Then there was this major explosion and all this stuff started falling. People around me started yelling and screaming and crying. I was in total shock."

Chris Donelly: "My girlfriend and I were talking on the cell phone. I was on my way to meet someone at Lehman Brothers. I looked up in the sky. I could see the jet. It looked like it was going to smash right into the World Trade Center. Then it did. This big ball of fire burst out from the side of the building. Then all this smoke started pouring out and debris and papers began falling in a confetti-like cloud. People on the street started screaming, and sobbing, and pointing, and yelling 'no, no, no, no, no, no.' It was terrifying. Horrible. A nightmare."

Mercedes Darden was late and hurrying for work. She heard the sound of a jet. Mercedes was familiar with that sound. It was a Boeing. She had flown on one for years, having worked as a flight attendant before getting married.

"Right away I knew something was wrong. It was too loud. Then everything became dream-like. All the pigeons in the street flew up just as I was looking up. I saw the jet just as it hit the tower. The tower rippled at first. Shimmered. Vibrated. You could see the vibration waves rolling down toward the ground."

Patrick O'Conner: "I could hear the jet. It was very loud. It was unusual. You normally don't hear a jet like that down here. I shaded my eyes and there it was. It was way too low. It was headed straight for the tower, like the pilot was going to try to fly right through the building. Then, wham. Boom. You could see the concussion move up and down the building, then the smoke and debris falling like spaghetti toward the ground."

Within seconds, crowds began to gather on the sidewalk and in the street. Office workers. Store clerks. Pointing. Gesticulating. Yelling. Crying. Gaping at the incredible destruction

Billowing smoke and tongues of flame were roaring out of a huge ragged hole in the sides of the north tower.

From the street, it was impossible to see all the trapped people who were gathering at the busted out windows, gasping for air, trying to escape the flames.

Dozens of people, then dozens more began crowding the broken windows of the upper floors, climbing out, standing on the window's edge, some even trying to climb down to safety. It was the same on every side of the tower.

The heat was incredibly intense. The suffocating clouds of black smoke were making it impossible to breathe. Massive amounts of jet fuel were ablaze and setting everything on fire. The building itself began to melt.

On the upper floors, right above the site of impact, dozens of people pounded on the narrow windows, smashing furniture, their bodies, anything against the stubborn glass, trying to smash their way through, for air, to breath, for a last gasp of life.

Those who had found broken windows, and had climbed upon the ragged sills, now had nowhere else to go. Colleagues and friends crowded up beside them. Dozens, hundreds more had fallen behind them, overcome by the heat and the smoke.

They started leaping and falling from the upper floors. There was no other escape.

Many couldn't control their own movements. The heat was unbearable. They were forced to leap. The heat was too intense, the flames licking at their skins. The choice was no choice at all, either burn alive or jump.

Some tried to climb down from the broken windows, to shimmy down alongside the outside of the tower, hoping to reach safety on a lower floor.

But the tower itself was melting. The temperature of the steel and glass tower was rapidly climbing to beyond a thousand degrees. They couldn't hold on because their hands were on fire. They were forced to let go. They fell.

Some managed to climb down, alongside the building, down they went two or three floors. But the fire was faster than they were. A few hung precariously but the heat was too intense. These brave souls flipped backward, falling, flailing their arms, down into the concrete abyss.

From the street, you could see what looked like dark lumps falling along the side of the building. Many of the onlookers were not sure what they were seeing.

What they were seeing were people: Men and women jumping and leaping out of the broken windows.

Sarah Sampino couldn't take her eyes off the 85th floor. Smoke was billowing from the windows. "I use to work on that floor," she said. Now her old office was in flames and there were people jumping from the 85th floor to their death.

A policeman arrived on the scene and was paralyzed by the sight. "People were actually jumping right in front of us. One after another, just splattering."

What would it be like? One moment, you are sitting in your office, high above Manhattan, having coffee, kidding with friends, checking your e-mail, and the next minute you are free-falling from the 80th floor.

"This has got to be a dream," you might have said. "This has got to be a nightmare. This is not happening. Wake up! Wake up!"

As you fell, time itself would slow down to an eternity. If you were not badly burned or in pain, you would have time to think, to reflect, to even experience memory flash backs, a life review: Your entire life flashing before your eyes as you hurtled to the ground.

Many of those who have been in traumatic situations where their lives are in incredible danger, often report that everything slows down, they enter a realm of delayed motion.

Many who face certain death, and live to tell the tail, report seeing their entire lives flash before their eyes... and because time slows down to an eternity, they have time to remember every important event, from childhood to the point of impact: A birthday party, the first day at school, a favorite teacher, mom and dad, that first kiss, on and on, every memory; even the ancient Egyptians referred to these experiences, called the life review.

Some who face death and are involved in horrific accidents, experience themselves as splitting off from their bodies, as if they are hovering upon the ceiling staring down at themselves: a phenomenon referred to as dissociation in which the mind literally splits in half. They see themselves from afar, as if looking at a snap shot of themselves, similar to watching an actor on a movie screen. They are both the actor and the audience and experience themselves as two different people, one passively watching, the other being observed.

One woman stated: "It was though I were two persons, one watching, and the other having this happen to me."

Another said: "I had a clear image of myself... as though watching it on a television screen."

Lisa, 22, who lost her arm in an auto accident, recalls that after she collapsed to the ground, the next thing she noticed was that she was up in the air looking down at her body, and from above, she could see the ambulance crew working, picking up her body, placing it on a gurney and into the ambulance.

Nor is the experience frightening. Rather, the victim may feel at peace, and experience a very pleasant sensation of elation.

Some of those who have survived near death experiences, have also reported that things suddenly became "crystal clear" or that they had a feeling of clairvoyance, of having the truth revealed to them, of having achieved a sense of greater awareness such that sounds, smells and visual objects seemed to have a greater meaning and sensibility.

Approximately 37% of patients who die and are then revived report similar experiences.

Consider, for example, the case of Army Specialist J. C. Bayne of the 196th Light Infantry Brigade who had been machine gunned and struck by a mortar during the Viet Nam War. According to Bayne, when he opened his eyes he was floating in the air, looking down on his burnt and bloody body: "I could see me... it was like looking at a manikin laying there... I was burnt up and there was blood all over the place... I could see the Vietcong. I could see the guy pull my boots off. I could see the rest of them picking up various things... I was like a spectator...

It was about four or five in the afternoon when our own troops came. I could hear and see them approaching... I looked dead... they put me in a bag... transferred me to a truck and then to the morgue...and I could see that too..."

Those who leaped, or fell or who were sucked out of the upper floors of the burnings towers may have also had a disassociating experience as they fell. They were not only falling, but observing themselves falling.... hovering above and taking it all in.

One can only hope that as they fell they were at peace, that they experienced only pleasant memories during that eternity of space that stretched from the upper floors to certain death below.

And they fell. By the dozens they fell. Some even held hands.

The people on the street could only gasp and cry.

Then, a second plane appeared in the sky.

Some have speculated the 18 minute delay between attacks was purposeful. The attacks were staggered to give the media an opportunity to set up their cameras and have them focused on the towers so as to capture the second "triumphant" attack: to make a recording of a horrifying event that would torture the mind for all eternity. This way the trauma could be relived over and over and over again, and whatever message the terrorists meant to send could be experienced forever.

"This was staged like it was a TV show. It was meant to be right before our eyes," said Joan Deppa, a Syracuse University professor and expert on the media and disasters.

When the second plane appeared in the sky, people on the streets began to panic. Many cried and sobbed. Many others wisely began to run.

The jetliner banked upward and flew directly into the south tower, picking a location somewhat below that chosen for the north Tower. There was a huge fireball and the upper floors exploded. A rainfall of debris, glass and pieces of human bodies were cast into the air and tossed down to the ground. Metal and concrete casing the size of boulders landed in the street, crushing and maiming those down below.

Scott was getting ready to leave his apartment, which was just 3 blocks south of the World Trade Center. "I heard what I thought was an explosion. A few seconds after, I could hear lots of debris hitting the building and I thought that maybe a car bomb had gone off. I finished getting dressed and went outside. I was still thinking "car bomb" and walked north to the corner and there was a human hand on the ground. Someone quickly threw a coat over it. That's when I looked up and saw that the north tower had a big burning hole at the top of it."

"All of a sudden, I heard the sound of an airplane and looked up to see a commercial jet slam right into the south tower. I was probably only 200 yards from the base of the building and watched the plane come in, hit the building and explode. All of a sudden it was like a movie scene, where everyone just turned and were literally running for their lives."

Cars and trucks came to a halt. Men and women bolted from their vehicles and ran for their lives. People were running, crying and screaming. An empty baby stroller sat abandoned in the plaza. Dozens of abandoned handbags, shoes, backpacks and bicycles littered the streets.

Men and women ran for their lives down Vesey Street. Waves of screaming people stampeded down Church St., looking for anywhere to hide.

The skies were filled with flames and billowing smoke. On the ground lay broken glass, shiny metal...and human bodies. Bodies, some flung from the upper stories, some killed by falling debris lay here and there along the sidewalks and the street. A bicycle messenger lay on his side, the torso of a man lay nearby.

Richard Micok worked on the 50th floor with a bonds trader, but had gone out to get some bagels and coffee. "I turned around and saw the plane heading toward the building...I saw the explosion... I rushed back. My friends were inside! On the ground I saw bodies and flesh just lying around like a slaughterhouse. I will never forget the sight of a burning corpse or the stench of burning flesh."

Some of civilians on the upper floors of the south tower, who had been watching the unfolding drama taking place in the adjacent tower, now they too were victims, and they began to leap and jump in order to escape the roaring flames.

Dozens of desperate men and women, trapped by searing flames gathered at the broken windows of the south Tower and stared out into the abyss, hoping beyond hope that they might be rescued alive. But there was no escape. They were a thousand feet up. The raging fires were roaring toward them.

One by one, they plunged from the top floors of the towers...doing anything and everything to escape the roaring hell that was bearing down on them.

In the minutes before the second jet hit, some of the occupants of the south tower had already packed their things, intending to leave, and some were already in the elevator, on their way to safety and home. But for too many, it was too late.

Those riding the elevators were enveloped in a sea of flames. Those on the upper floors where the second jetliner struck—their offices had become flaming graves.

******

"The whole building moved and it was swaying back and forth. I heard a muffled boom and I thought everything was just going to collapse. People were rushing and merging together and going crazy."

The floor began to tremble. The windows cracked and fell. There were periodic eruptions. On some floors, giant fire balls burst out of the walls. Bodies were helplessly tumbling out of the upper floors, many of them in flames.

Most of those inside the towers, particularly those in offices on the lower floors, felt the impact of the crash but had no idea what happened. But for many of those on the upper floors, the impact was horrendous and they instantly realized their lives were in mortal danger.

Those who were working on the 90th floor heard an incredible deafening explosion which shook the upper building with such intensity that those standing were thrown to the floor. So much debris instantly filled the air, that almost everyone realized they had to leave. But many couldn't because they had been hurt, or couldn't find the way out. There was so much debris and so much smoke that it was almost impossible to see or to breathe.

Chris, who was visiting with his girlfriend on the 90th floor, felt what he thought was an earthquake. "It was like some kind of giant serpent slithered beneath the floor, making the floors swell up and then sway back and forth. My girlfriend panicked. I told her, 'Let's get out of here.' We went out into the hall and it was already starting to fill with smoke. The stairwells too were filling up with smoke. Smoke was seeping up from the bottom floors."

Those seeking to escape the chaos and the ever present threat of death, made their way down emergency staircases and then poured into the interconnection concourse that links the two towers at ground level.

There were several stairwells to choose from. On some, there was panic. On another, there was no escape.

On yet another, the escape was orderly but painfully, frightfully slow. As recalled by one survivor: "I was at the tail end of the crowd. You wait. People are orderly. It's crowded and it's slow. You go down a few steps and it would stop. Some of the stops were five minutes. You don't know why."

B.J.B. recalls that he had just come back from a meeting at 7:30 a.m. in the neighboring World Financial Center building where he used to work, when he was with Merrill Lynch. His office was on the 38th floor of the World Trade Center:

"I had just come back and was sitting at my desk for about ten minutes before I heard and felt the first attack. I heard a thunderous BOOM and then felt the jostling and swaying of the WTC

1 building. The feeling was something akin to someone grabbing you by the shoulders and swinging you back and forth a few times."

"Startled, I looked out the window just a few feet away to see glass, thousands of sheets of paper and large metal pieces raining down from above. My first thought was that the top of the building blew off by some gas explosion or that a plane or helicopter had clipped the top of the building."

"For a brief moment, I had the impulse to get closer to the window and look out. Then, I had second thoughts. I grabbed my wallet, keys and Palm Pilot (they were right in front of me) and ran to the emergency stairwell."

"It's funny how nobody really knows where the stairwell is until something like this happens. I finally found it."

"It took me 40 minutes to get down. The stairs were narrow and only wide enough for people to walk down two abreast. Several times, the flow of people-traffic stopped."

"We started seeing lots of smoke."

"Around the 19th floor, the firemen, running up the stairs, passed by with the look of uncertainty in their eyes. Water started rushing down the stairs like a river flooding the floors further below."

"At this point, nobody knew what was going on. No one knew a jet had struck the tower. No one knew that terrorists had hijacked a jet and committed suicide by striking the World Trade Center. We had no idea how serious the situation was. The people on the lower floors had no idea as to why exactly they were abandoning the building, and I don't think the people on the upper floors had much time to think about it."

"It was hot. The temperature in the stairwell was rising due to the amount of people trying to get out. It was nerve wracking. The sounds of men and women getting nervous didn't help the people trying to cling to their sanity."

"Finally, we had made it to the lobby. I was one of the lucky ones because I was only on the 38th floor. There were still a lot of people trying to get out."

"I could hear the sound of stuff falling outside. It was raining broken glass, debris and things that were burning."

"The sight of one of the tallest buildings in the world in flames, made me feel terrified."

"A lot of people were running. I joined them. We were headed towards a covered bridge that runs between the WTC and the World Financial Center (across the West Side Highway, going towards the water). That's when I began to see the bodies...bodies on the ground, bodies that were still falling. I can tell you, that is one thing that you never want to see is someone falling 80 stories to the ground."

There were over 5000 people in each tower. Thousands were trying to escape. The stairs became increasingly crowded. Heat began to build from the fires that raged up above. Water was pouring down the stairwells and all the while the building was creaking and cracking, and it felt like it was coming apart.

As related by Sandra Gonzales: "All the way down it felt like the ground was falling out from under you. I knew the building had been severely damaged and all the way down you could feel that it was about to collapse. Then the lights went dark. That scared me almost to death. I just wanted out of there."

John Labriola started a new contract for the Port Authority about two weeks prior to the attack on the World Trade Center. His personal account on the morning of September 11: "I drove in that day down the East River Drive and parked in a lot three blocks south of WTC 2. I started taking pictures. The light was beautiful that morning. At 8:05 am I took a photo of the Trade Center and the Greek Orthodox Church that shares the lot with the parking lot, just south of WTC 2."

"The Port Authority had given me a cubicle on the south side of the 71st floor in the north tower of the World Trade Center. At 8:30 a.m. I was in a status meeting on 71 East. Suddenly, the building rocked and then swayed first in one direction then shuddered back and forth at least five or six feet in each direction and finally settled. None of us were hurt or knocked off our seats, but getting up while the building was moving was difficult."

"From the conference room door I could see out the window. The sky was so blue. Papers were flying everywhere. It looked like a ticker tape parade. We were on the east side of the building. We speculated from the start that we were hit by a plane. I ran around the floor to the south side of the building, grabbed my backpack and laptop. Everyone was off the floor pretty quickly. I, and the guy I report to, headed out to the lobby."

"One of the stairwells smelled strongly of smoke, so we avoided that one. The other seemed okay and we joined a group who were headed down. We walked down two by two stopping every so often for some unknown reason. Some people were helped down from higher floors with terrible burns over their bodies. Whenever necessary, we would press ourselves into a single file line to let the people, who had been badly burned and injured, get by.

"It was pretty hot; people were slipping on the sweat of the people who had come before them. In some places, the smoke was worse than others. People covered their mouths and eyes with whatever they had available. A fellow who had been on the 81st floor told me his floor was set on fire immediately after the first plane struck."

"We were still climbing down the stairs when the second plane struck. We felt it, but had no idea what it was. It wasn't until someone began getting news on his pager that we knew that a plane had hit each of the towers and the Pentagon. People were constantly checking their cell phones to see if there was service. Many of us had service, but no calls could get out. I remember joking that we should all buy stock in the first company whose service worked."

"Around the 35th floor, we started meeting a steady stream of firefighters walking up and had to press into single file again. None of them said a word as they went up and past us carrying unbelievable loads of equipment. They were already exhausted by the time we started seeing them. I can't stop thinking about the look in their eyes and how heroic they were. I pray some of them made it out."

"As we continued down the stairwells, water started pouring down the steps. This got worse as we got lower down. The stairwell led down to an outside door lined with emergency workers who were urging us to move to safety. The courtyard where this outdoor landing led us onto must have been blocked or too dangerous for us to cross because we were directed back into that second floor balcony again and down two escalators into the mall under Tower 1."

"Water was falling everywhere - 8 to 10 inches in some places. Many of the stores had their windows blown out. All along the way emergency workers urged us to keep moving. I went up another escalator in the northeast corner of the mall and out onto Church Street."

"Finally, I was outside; it took 50 minutes in all to get down. As I stepped into the light, emergency workers were yelling, "Don't look up, keep moving!" I crossed the street and tilted my head upwards. It was unreal. I saw someone fall from Tower 1. I stopped looking up."

"I looked at the ground around us and there was a lot of blood. Some shrapnel caught my attention. I couldn't stop thinking that it must have been from the plane. Shoes where everywhere, newspapers and blood. When I looked up, the people I was with were gone."

Eric S. Levine was on the 64th Floor. "I was sitting at my computer reading the BBC on the Internet when I heard an explosion. I ran to a window and looked out to see large amounts of debris —papers, metal, all kinds of things— floating down towards the street. Someone called out to me, 'Is there anyone down there?' 'Yes!' I said and he yelled at me to, 'Get your ass into the stairwell because we are evacuating!'"

"At first, people were still very calm and were evacuating in an orderly fashion. We had reached either the 51st or the 50th floor when we heard a huge explosion, which shook the building like crazy! I grabbed hold of the stairwell to steady myself. A woman actually fell down on top of me and knocked me down. I tried to stand up but the building was still shaking and the lights were flickering on and off. It was terrifying!"

"Then, the building began to sink - that's the only way I can describe it. The floor began to lower under your feet and all I could think about was that it would crack open and I would fall hundreds of feet to my death!"

"Until this moment no one knew what was going on and no one was really scared yet. Everyone thought the problem was in 1 WTC, the other tower. Not in our tower. Once the building felt like it was sinking and started to shake, everything just turned into pandemonium! People began screaming and crying and praying out loud for God to help them. People were panicking and a stampede started and they were running each other down."

"Myself and the Philippine woman who had landed on me and a few other people, waited for the initial surge of panicked people to subside. We began to move down the stairwell again. Somewhere between the 44th and 34th floors I lost sight of the little Philippine woman who had been hanging onto my arm for dear life. She was there one moment and gone the next. This really bothers me a lot. I can't help but wonder what happened to her."

"Around the 25th floor we began to smell jet fuel. There was a lot of it. I have asthma and it became difficult to breathe. By the 15th floor, it became unbearable due to the amount of smoke that was now entering the stairwell. So I took off my shirt and wrapped it around my head to help me breathe and it worked, but my eyes were stinging real bad."

"It took about 40 minutes to get down that stairwell. We were met by rescue people, firemen, and cops who were asking if anyone needed medical attention and then yelling at you to keep moving towards the escalators. I don't think those guys got out."

"I remember that when we were about to get on the escalators, you could look out the windows onto the square between the two buildings. I could see the large ball sculpture and the fountain and lots and lots of bodies— some were still falling to the ground and some still smoldering. I will never forget that sight as long as I live."

As employees working at the World Trade Center made their mad dash for safety and ran into the streets, most were stunned to see how deadly the situation really was and just how much their lives had been in jeopardy. Clouds of smoke filled the air. Debris and broken glass were everywhere. People were crying and weeping in hysterics. Everything, everyone was covered in soot. There were bodies and body parts everywhere.

One young woman turned and looked up just in time to see a body fall from the tower she had just escaped.

An associate producer for Fox News Channel who had just arrived at the base of the World Trade Center said, "I saw people falling out of the building from the top. People in ties and jackets, free-falling backwards with their hands out. It looked like they were parachuting, but without the parachutes."

Martin, a college student, who was there to meet a friend, looked up into the smoked filled skies only to witness "people literally jumping off or falling off the towers. It was like a weird unbelievable nightmare. It was surreal. Maybe I imagined it, but I thought I could hear people screaming in torment as they fell."

Some stood and stared. But many panicked and ran for their lives. It was pure frenzy..

Michael Stock had been riding the escalator from the train station when the jet hit. There was an immediate stampede for safety, though many stopped to stare.

As recalled by Stock: "I stood in the doorway where the train station meets the street. From the doors you were able to see lots and lots of debris falling. The first decision was: do you cross the street to get away from the debris? But on the other hand, thousands were running. Would I be killed by the stampede? Luckily, when I was running, most of the debris was paper stuff."

Triage units were set up out in the open, next to the Trade Center in front of the Hilton Millennium Hotel on Church Street. Office workers who had escaped the damaged buildings, but with severe burns and injuries, sat on the sidewalk as blood and puss streamed from open wounds.

There was a woman in a slinky black dress, her face covered in blood. There was a man wearing the remnants of a smoldering three piece suit, his face red, scarred and puffy. The hair was burnt from his face and head.

A young woman lay curled in a ball, crying hysterically.

Another sat staring mutely, her body half naked and burnt.

A young man wearing a black spandex bicycle messenger outfit lay on the ground cursing and nursing a broken leg.

A few feet away, a heavyset woman was plumped on the sidewalk, shaking uncontrollably, her hair caked in blood and breathing through an inhaler as a rescue worker attended her wounds.

And strewn upon the ground were the body parts. A naked leg with its foot inside a shiny shoe. A bone with grizzled muscle and chunks of hairy skin.

"I saw body parts," said attorney John Fulweiler whose hair, face and suit were covered with dust. "I looked down and saw this hunk of flesh."

Meanwhile, people kept streaming out of the buildings as more rescue workers and firefighters raced in.

Many believed the worst was over and stopped to rest and congratulate themselves. It was time to tend their wounds, to catch their breath, and to thank god they were alive. True, there were people to be saved and fires to be fought, there were still people inside, thousands of people coming down the stairwell, but for those outside, the terror of the unknown was gone. They were bruised, battered and frightened, but they had got out. Thank god, they had escaped. Except for the pain of their injuries, and the emotional shock, the worst was over.

Many lingered. Some sat down to rest. Others waited for

treatment.

Firefighters, police, doctors and nurses, were doing what they do best.

No one suspected what was coming next.

******

10:04 am. The south Tower began to shudder. The upper floors seemed to list to the side.

Police officers on the scene may have been the first to realize what was about to happen. They began warning people to get up, to keep moving and to head north.

"The buildings may fall. Go. Run!" they urged.

But that was unthinkable. It was unimaginable.

The injured stayed put. The tired sat down. Those waiting to use the pay phone stayed in line. And rescuer workers, medical technicians, doctors, nurses and firemen continued to do their jobs: saving people, fighting fires and tending the injured. Most ignored the increasingly frantic warnings of the police.

10:05 a.m. It was at that moment that the south tower collapsed in a plume of ash and debris.

The south tower shook. There was a deafening, ear splitting, frightful roar and then the south tower began to lean further to the side and then implode upon itself. In dream-like slow motion it mushroomed in on itself and fell down down down to the ground.

Horror and catastrophe were raining down from the smoke covered sky. Glass and aluminum sheathing crashed to the pavement, crushing, maiming and killing those down below.

As described by one survivor: "It was horrifying. It was just unreal. The building went down, almost in slow motion and a black gray cloud just spread over lower Manhattan."

The cloud began expanding, growing larger, rising upward and then downward, swallowing the streets and all in its path as it sped uptown. People began running, running, chased down the canyons of the city by the blinding gray-black storm—this tornado of dust and ash. Then, everything turned black.

The forceful wind unleashed by the collapsing tower blew Linda Lorenz across the street, onto the hood of a car. There was so much smoke and debris she was unable to see. She could barely breathe. She rolled off the car and discovered the door was ajar. She slid inside, but it was already filled with dust. "I was choking on dust. On this gray grime. I was dry-heaving and kept spitting up this thick black gunk. It was awful. I felt like I was drowning."

After escaping from the north tower, John Labriola decided to head south down Broadway toward his car.

"The doors to Trinity Church were open so I stepped inside. A priest was leading a prayer service; I knelt to say a prayer. That was when the south tower fell. There was an incredible explosion. You could feel it as much as hear the building collapse. The stained glass church windows that had been filled with color and light turned inky black. Debris hit the roof of the church. People dove under pews. I looked out the front door. I couldn't see three feet in front of me. I thought, "It must be impossible to breathe outside."

"We gathered everyone inside the church, searched for and found some water and food. We made up wet towels if, for any reason, we had to leave the protection of the church, and needed protection to breath. We waited for the air outside to be clear enough to see. Someone found a radio and positioned it on a pulpit."

"It grew lighter outside the church. And then, the second building fell. Blackness again. Larger objects were hitting the roof of the church."

"Outside, it was a mess. Winds would whip through the streets causing temporary white outs and blacking out the sun. Emergency vehicles caused their own white outs and you would have to hide your face as they came by."

"The group I left with headed south, then east, then north. All along the way, people were gathered in disbelief. Radios drew large crowds. I remember someone talking on a cell phone telling his friend that no one above the 60th floor could have gotten out. I told him that that wasn't true, I had walked down from 71. He called after me, "'Thank you Sir. Thank you.'"

******

The towers were doomed to collapse, not only because the impact of the two hijacked jets, but because of the incredible intensity of the fires.

Even after the jets struck, no one suspected the Twin Towers, with their unique steel and concrete architecture could possibly collapse. More than 200,000 tons of steel and 425,000 cubic yards of concrete went into creating the structures. They were built to withstand almost any kind of conceivable punishment.

As pointed out by Hyman Brown, a University of Colorado civil engineering professor and the Trade Center's construction manager, the Twin Towers were in fact constructed so they could withstand the direct force of an airline crash. Because of their height, this was factored in during their construction. It was always a possibility that an accident could occur. "But steel melts, and 24,000 gallons of aviation fluid melted the steel. Nothing is designed or will be designed to withstand that kind of fire," Brown pointed out.

Almost all experts are in agreement: No feat of architecture could withstand the power of these two hammer blows and an ensuing raging hellish fire.

The hammer blows and the raging fires made the collapse inevitable. The towers had to have been weakened by the initial impact of each jet. But it was the heat of the raging fires, ignited by the jet's leaking petrol, which sealed the towers' fate.

Steel melts.

Each jet carried over 24,000 gallons of aviation fuel. Once these were set ablaze, temperatures rose to above 20,000 degrees. It would be impossible for any building to resist those temperatures.

However, when it comes to intense heat and an ensuing total collapse, the 1400 foot Twin Towers were particularly vulnerable.

In constructing the Twin Towers, the designers wished to provide the maximum possible amount of office area. They wanted lots of space and this could be achieved by eliminating the interior support columns. Interior columns are normally a standard feature of almost all skyscrapers.

Instead, interior columns were replaced by an exterior core-tubular steel columns, which would hold not just the walls up but the floors as well.

Once the tubular steel columns that ringed the building began to melt, the attached floors became detached. That floor would fall, striking the floor below, which was also weakened by the heat.

Each massive floor collapsed and caved into the one below it, like a domino effect.

As the floors collapsed one by one, they created a chimney at the center of the building, allowing the fires to grow to even greater intensities. Finally, one floor, then another and another, began to fall, causing the entire tower to implode all the way down to the ground floor.

Thousands were killed who had stayed in the buildings, thinking that the danger had passed. Hundreds more were killed who were still descending the stairways. Hundreds more who were out front when it collapsed, including firemen, police, rescue workers, doctors, nurses, the curious and the injured, were buried alive and crushed.

******

For those who escaped and survived the collapsing towers, timing was everything. There was only a brief moment before the window of opportunity slammed shut, killing those who had lingered or were left behind.

"If I didn't leave the minute I did," said Thomas Lochtefeld, "I'd be dead."

It took many of the survivors working between the 80th and 105th floors of the north and south towers, as long as an hour to make it down the stairs and to the ground floors. Many were just exiting the buildings when the south tower collapsed. There were hundreds, perhaps thousands more, still inside trying anything and everything to escape.

As reported by one survivor, Kim White: "We were up the escalator about to go out the door when the building collapsed."

Others died because they ran back inside to rescue or help a beloved friend or dear colleague.

Some believe this was the fate of John Hart. John had escaped the fires consuming the upper floors, had dodged the advancing flames and made it down the stairwell, only to turn back at the last moment to save a friend.

"Someone got a report that they saw him come out of the building and then go back in to help someone, which would totally be John."

After the first jet struck, and prior to the collapse of the south Tower, thousands of office workers had begun to evacuate. However, when they heard an announcement urging them to return to work, thousands returned to their offices and certain death.

Mike Shillaker, had traveled from England and was at the World Trade Center on business. "We were on the 72nd floor of WTC 2 when the first plane hit Tower 1 - we heard the bang, and saw debris. Thank god, the client that I and my colleague were visiting had the sense to realize what was going on. He told us to get out of the building."

They ran for their lives.

"As we got to around floor 50, a message came over the loudspeakers, telling us that there was an isolated fire in Tower 1, and we did not need to evacuate Tower 2. Again, thank god we continued down. Others didn't."

"As we reached around floor 38, the second plane hit. We escaped. We were very lucky: many, many others, I know—were not so lucky. As we ran, the vivid picture of streams and streams of firefighters traveling towards the scene will stick in my mind forever. As we were escaping, they were heading straight towards a total disaster area - and I think even then, we realized that many of those men and women would probably not return alive."

For many of those who returned or remained in their offices on the upper floors, and for those who were trapped above the carnage and destruction left by the hijacked planes, there was no escape. Once the jets struck, there was no way out.

John Hart was working on the top floors of the south Tower. His job was to help integrate computer systems with a recently merged company. When the first jet struck, he called his wife Laurie to tell her what happened and then reassured her he was safe. He called her back 20 minutes later, after the second jet barreled into the floors beneath his own.

"Laurie," he said, "I've got big problems." In the background she could hear people screaming. Then the line weant dead.

The second jet struck the 70th floors and careened into those above. Most of those working in these offices were instantly in-cinerated.

Many of those on the floors immediately above and beneath the site of impact were also doomed. There would be almost no opportunity to run, no chance to escape. They too would be con-sumed by smoke and flames.

There were flames everywhere. Giant balls of flames were bursting out of both sides of the tower. It was a raging inferno fueled by the jellied petroleum spilling from the guts of the jet. Several secondary fires began to erupt everywhere throughout the upper and lower floors.

When a fire starts inside a building, once the building struc-ture itself and the materials inside that building start to burn, the fires can race through the building faster than a person can run.

It was this raging inferno and the secondary explosions, which presumably ended the lives of hundreds, if not thousands of those on the upper levels of the north and south towers.

"It must have been hell," said firefighter Paul Curran of New York Fire Patrol 3. "There were a lot of jumpers. I saw bodies hit the upper level concrete of the second floor overhang of Tower One. Others were falling into West Street."

A giant fireball apparently consumed eight firemen from Ladder No. 5, the first firefighters to arrive upon the scene. One of these men, Mike Warchola, was retiring the next day. Another, Greg Saucedo, was expecting to be promoted to lieutenant.

But this was their job: To save people. And certainly all of these men knew with fatal certainty they might die. They could feel the heat, hear the secondary explosions and the crackle and roar of the flames. They could smell the gas, the fuel from the jet, they could see the orange red flames and the thick black smoke. They could also hear the screams, the blood curdling shrieks and the cries for help—and they pushed onwards. Whereas other men might run and hide, these men, these courageous, brave men, pushed onward, defying death, defying fear, marching through the gates of hell, because, because they were brave, because they were heroes, because that's what they were there for. That's what they were trained for. They were supermen.

They died trying to save lives, trying to save those who could not save themselves. They were brave, courageous, self-less heroes.

They were Americans!

******

The men of Ladder 24 and Ladder 5 pulled up in their trucks at the same time. Without hesitating, the men went straight up into the north tower. They climbed stairwell "A".

"We made it up 37 floors carrying a lot of heavy equipment," said Marcel Claes of Engine No. 24, "Then we got an urgent message to come right back down. I think the Ladder 5 guys may have proceeded up farther."

But in coming back down, Marcel became separated from

his buddies. He was directed to another stairwell on the sixth floor. "I manned my rig as the pump operator, but we ran out of water. I had to take care of that and get more water. I went back down and outside."

It just a few minutes the south Tower would fall killing all of the firemen who were climbing the stairs and still arriving to save the lives of those who were unable to save themselves.

Fire fighting unit, Ladder 7, got the call at 9:10 am and arrived in front of the south tower within minutes.

The men of Ladder 7 quickly entered the south tower and were on their way up the stairwells, lugging their gear, moving slowly, single file past the frightened civilians who were heading the other way.

They were making good progress, some of the survivors recalling they had passed these men on the 40th floor.

Within moments of the arrival of Ladder 7, Engine 16, arrived. As related by Firefighter Lieutenant Kross, although the south and north Towers were still standing, and no one had even conceived of the possibility they might fall, people were running, debris was falling, fires were billowing from the side of the towers, and it was utter chaos.

The men of Engine 16, and those of Ladder 24 and Ladder 5, made for the north tower and began lugging their heavy gear up the smoke filled stairways. Onward, upward, passed the frightened office workers who were hurrying to get away.

Kross was told to report to the fire chief who was on the 23rd floor of the north tower. Engine crew 16 followed close behind.

Kross and the chief began to confer, detailing the plan of attack when the building began to rumble.

"I thought it was an elevator falling to the ground."

It was the south tower.

Kross immediately ordered his men to evacuate.

It was not easy to get out of the north Tower. Perhaps as many as a thousand office workers had lingered, thinking the worst was over. But once the south tower fell, there was a mad scramble for life.

Everyone knew that the north Tower might be next.

It was pure pandemonium. A mass stampede down the stairwells. People climbed over each other, knocked each other down, trampled those who had fallen.

They had to get out!

They had to get out!

The south Tower had just fallen and everyone left alive inside the north tower knew that at any moment they might be next.

As related by Kross, who was still inside: "When we got down to the fourth floor there was the loudest rumble I've heard in my life. I grabbed my helmet over my head and made myself into a small ball."

All around him the world began to collapse.

"I thought I was going to die."

When Kross opened his eyes, he was covered with debris and in complete darkness. He was sure the north tower had collapsed on top of him. Slowly, cautiously, he sought to free himself from the rubble and found a small opening. He climbed through it only to fall down to the next floor, landing beside a battalion chief and another lieutenant.

"I thought we were totally buried and we remained huddled there so as to not dislodge more debris and bring more of the building down on us." But after about an hour, as the smoke and clouds of dust began to clear, they saw light and crawled to safety, only to discover that hundreds of their "brothers" had all been killed.

Dozens of rescue workers were killed while treating injured victims who had lingered for treatment after making the harrowing escape from the towers before they fell.

Temporary medical triage units and fire command posts had been established at the base of the south tower. Yet another had been set up beneath a bridge which enabled pedestrians to walk to and from the World Trade Center and the World Financial Center at 200 Liberty Street.

When the south tower collapsed, all those at the base were

instantly killed by falling debris, including high ranking officers who were directing the rescue operation. The bridge too was struck and also fell, killing those working beneath it.

THE SOUTH TOWER FALLS

Hundreds of rescuers, including New York City's finest-the NYPD, and Port Authority officers, were killed when the south and north towers collapsed.

Likewise, many of those seeking to escape these towering buildings also died because they were still inside or were unable to vacate quickly enough.

Many died because they lingered at the base of the World Trade Center, talking to friends, watching the firefighters and the unfolding drama or just waiting in line to use the pay phone. Every cell phone in New York City had stopped working. The phone signals had been coming from the top of what once were the Twin Towers.

As related by one survivor, Robert Mattox: "No one's cell phones were working and people were lined up at the pay phones. There were people crying hysterically. There were people needing to get in touch with their families."

Many of these people were killed by falling debris or suffocated in falling dust, when the south Tower collapsed. Even those standing at least a block away weren't safe from drowing in the tidal wave of dust.

Scott Matthews and his brother were visiting from California and were standing at least 100 yards away.

"All at once people started shouting and screaming, 'It's coming down. It's coming down!' And then there was this horrible roar. Me and my brother ran for our lives. Everybody was running, screaming. People were falling, tripping over each other and screaming. I still remember that roar and the screams. Even the men were screaming. I think even I was screaming. We ran for our lives. When we looked back, it was like it had been hit my an atomic bomb."

Firefighter Paul Curran of New York Fire Patrol 3, had just entered the lobby when the south Tower began to rumble and then disintegrate. "We all just ran," he said. "We couldn't do nothing but save ourselves. I got under a parked car with my respirator on. I was in total darkness for at least five minutes."

******

Many of the evacuees wanted to get as far away from the buildings as possible. Because they kept moving and because they continued walking north they were able to save themselves.

Michael Stork had made it to Battery Park when the first tower collapsed.

"I heard it before it fell. It sounded like an explosion, a bomb. People began running again....and then as it collapsed, it was like a whiteout in a blizzard, you couldn't see anything from all the ash."

Stork was covered with dust and ash. "Everybody's hair was covered in gray. My shoes were covered in gray. My glasses were covered. I saw it on my hands. Felt it on my hair. In my eyes."

Martin, an art student, had lingered, fearing for the safety of his friends. "There was a loud rumbling and everybody began running and ducking for cover as the south Tower collapsed...then it was just pure blackness. The air was filled with dust and dark smoke. I could see nothing. I was on the ground. Something had hit me and had thrown me against a wall. I thought I was dead."

According to rescue worker Trina Lopez, "When the tower collapsed, people were screaming and running, and all this stuff was barreling down the streets; this giant cloud, like an avalanche of dust and debris, white powder, soot, papers...and this huge gray cloud, like it was alive... like we were in this blinding storm. It just covered everything until everything turned pitch black, and so thick, you could hardly breathe."

"It was like a blizzard, like a tornado. It had that kind of power. It knocked me down and blew me face first underneath a car," reported Gilbert Rios.

"It was a rolling black cloud ten stories tall, coming at you and building speed. You couldn't see. You couldn't breathe. You couldn't outrun it."

Allison Keyes, a WCBS radio reporter, was interviewing rescue workers when the tower began to collapse. "The police said, 'Run.' And everybody ran. You could hear the building falling behind you. I looked back once and saw bricks flying and then this huge cloud of smoke and dust," she said. "My eyes were open, but it was like you were in a dark room."

When the south tower began to implode, people began running, screaming, yelling. It was a stampede of terrified people. It was mass hysteria. Those who fell were trampled to death or crushed and suffocated, by the billowing clouds of ash and falling debris.

To Scott, "it looked like a demolition explosion because it blew out in all directions and the top quarter just started to fall downward."

"Everyone was pretty much paralyzed for a second or two as we watched it fall and then I think we all realized that a massive cloud of debris was heading our way. People were jumping into the river."

"I sprinted to the closest building I saw, which turned out to be a restaurant with a large glass wall facing the river. I was pressed against the glass with a few other people when the cloud of debris finally came over the building. The air quickly got pretty thick full of ash. I took my shirt off and wrapped it around my face and head and started banging on the window with 2 other guys trying to figure out how to get into the restaurant. I could barely breathe, let alone see. My eyes were on fire."

Many of those who were close to the falling towers were smothered to death. They drowned in dust. Emergency Medical Service workers reported discovering dozens of bodies buried beneath two feet of soot.

Emergency Medical Service worker Louis Garcia, reported that were "bodies are all over the place, all buried beneath the soot. There's two feet of soot everywhere and a lot of the vehicles are running over bodies because they are all over the place."

Others were killed by the falling debris, including Rev. Mychal Judge, 68, known as "Father Mike." Father Mike, a 68-year-old Franciscan priest, had been serving as the FDNY's chaplain for ten years.

Judge was one of the first to arrive on the scene of the disaster and proceeded to give last rites to a firefighter, who lay dying after a body falling from the Towers struck him.

And then, as he gave last rites, Father Mike too was hit when the south Tower collapsed. He was killed while on his knees, praying for the firefighter's soul.

Later, it was said at his eulogy that he had died in order to be on the other side of death, there to greet the fallen firefighters.

A police officer with the NYPD, the brother of Ray Charles an emergency medical technician, was one of the officers killed when the south tower crumbled, crushing those down below.

"A lot of people got smashed. Just look around," Charles said, pointing out the shattered wreckage. "The ground here is covered with destroyed and smashed fire equipment. There's breathing apparatus, defibrillators, oxygen tanks and fire hoses."

"They lost some of their chiefs today," said Ray Kiernan, Chief of the New Rochelle Fire Department.

"They have to feel terribly. Dozens of guys were in there. The loss is going to be terrible."

After the south tower collapsed, firefighters began a Herculean effort to save their "brothers."

They dove into the hot smoldering wreckage.

"They were just tearing metal apart with their bare hands, trying to get there, to get them out," said Tracy Kraus, an emergency medical technician.

It is because of their heroic efforts to save their colleagues because they refused to turn back, that so many of them died when the second tower collapsed.

"More than 300 firefighters were killed," reported Fire Commissioner Thomas Von Essen.

Three top fire department officials, including Ray Downey, Chief of Special Operations Command, were killed. Downey, 63, was on the job for 39 years. Two out of his five children are firefighters. In 1995, Chief Downey led a team of New York firefighters to Oklahoma City after the bombing of the Alfred P. Murrah Federal Building.

"It is unimaginable, devastating, unspeakable carnage," said firefighter Scott O'Grady. "To say it looks like a war zone and to tell you about bodies lying in the street and blood and steel beams blocking roads would not begin to describe what it's like. It's horrible."

"I must have come across body parts by the thousands," said Angelo Otchy, a rescuer from the National Guard.

"You know what haunts me?" said Pete Genova. "There had to be 200 firemen that passed us on our way down. God only knows how many were up there when it collapsed."

More than 300 firefighters had lost their lives.

After the south tower fell, rescue workers, police officers and firemen attacked the rubble, tearing through the plaster and bent metal, looking for survivors, colleagues and friends. Firefighters searched for their "brothers"—men they had shared meals with, whose wives and families they knew, whose homes they had visited. The men buried beneath the rubble were their brethren and they dug until their hands were bleeding and raw.

"Everyone was hoping to find someone alive and pull him out," said retired fire fighter, Stephen Sullivan, the next day. "You hope. But you're afraid too, of what you'll find."

And so they dug. They could hear cries. Calls for help. Victims buried beneath the rubble were calling on their cell phones, pleading, begging for help.

But the nightmare was not yet over.

10:28 am. The north Tower of the World Trade Center collapsed.

And again, they ran. Again they stampeded. Cops, firemen, rescue workers, and the walking wounded; they panicked and people tripped, and people fell as they ran for their lives.

Again, more rescuers, firefighters, doctors, nurses and victims were suffocated or killed by the falling debris.

Hundreds of rescue workers were instantly killed. Mountains of soot and ash again tore through the city's narrow downtown streets, blanketing everything and everyone in inches of suffocating dust. Thousands of people were swallowed up as day turned into night and then into hell as the north Tower thundered down to the ground.

Instead of two towers, now there were none. Only angry plumes of thick gray-black clouds of smoke hung in the air for hours, visible even from outer space.

The mighty towers of the World Trade Center were humbled and reduced to nothing but a mountain of rubble.

And then, the people began to realize: The world was no longer safe. Every sound, every rumble and every creak was cause for alarm.

There was a plane overhead.

Was it going to crash into another building?

There was a helicopter.

Had it been hijacked?

Two jets streaked by in the distance.

Were they friend or foe?

"I feel like I am going to vomit," said 22 year-old Heather West. "I take careful breaths, disturbed, aware that I am breathing in the smoke and the physical remains of what was the World Trade Center. I was crying earlier. I do not know what to think or to feel. I peek my head out of the window of my bedroom in this dilapidated Brooklyn loft and glance towards the eerie twilight of Manhattan across the river. Greenish, ash-colored smoke still rises."

"A feeling of disjunction and uncertainty eats at my mind, disables my actions and kills my volition to do anything. We have clearly suffered a grievous hurt, and it is extremely unsettling. It is like having your guts pulled out—watching such a structure fall to its ruin, pompous and almost ridiculous in its enormity, a towering symbol of wealth, greed and competition—now a smoking void."

"I have become virtually paralyzed. I thought I could do anything, now I am unemployed, unsure of my future, soon to be without a home. My city and country have just been attacked. I watched the twin towers crumble before my eyes. I am dumbfounded and do not know how to react."

"Yesterday, I ventured into midtown to use a copy center and was struck by the silence. Some people stood on the edge of the sidewalk, pointing downtown towards the disaster site."

"All movement stopped for a moment as screaming sirens and a pack of squad cars approached, then disappeared down the gaping street. My heart raced for a moment and I joined the other bystanders to stare at the procession and wonder where they were going and what had happened."

"Anxiety was in the air. There was just too much space. The warm blanket of security has been ripped off our nation and we are left stark and feeling cold."

"I returned home, almost speed walking to the train. Burly NYPD officers awaited inside the stop, covering the entrances and leaning against the tunnel supports. Their presence incited more fear and worry than comfort and security. Inside the train I look at the faces crowding the car. Many heads were just fixated on the ground, despondent and speechless. We are all afraid."

THE BUCKET BRIGADES

Mayor Rudolph Giuliani publicly urged New Yorkers to stay calm and stay put, but, "If you're south of Canal Street, get out," he warned. "Just walk north."

Thousands of dazed New Yorkers did not need a warning. A massive exodus was taking place and citizens sought to flee Manhattan by any means possible: by boat, by foot, by offering cab drivers a thousand dollars for a 20 mile ride.

Bridges and highways were closed to all but emergency vehicles. In parts of the city, the subway system was shut down. The streets were grid-locked and motorists abandoned their stranded vehicles, joining the frantic exodus.

According to one onlooker, who boarded a ferry for safety: "As the boat pulled away from Manhattan, I could hardly believe what I was seeing. It looked like the entire downtown section of Manhattan was on fire. There was just a massive tower of smoke rising from the ashes."

Most of those who left the city that afternoon, like Lot's wife, couldn't help but look back at the destruction of the city. Towering pillars of smoke were rising from World Trade Center grave. It was a horrifying sight to behold.

And, like Lot's wife, they looked as if their bodies had been turned to pillars of salt, for thousands of those fleeing Manhatten that day had been covered with ash and soot.

For the next 12 hours, a steady stream of ferries and tugboats would disgorge the "walking wounded" and those lucky enough to have escaped injury.

"Every 10 minutes another boat with 100 to 150 people on it pulls up," said Mayor Glenn Cunningham.

All afternoon and into evening, they disgorged hundreds and hundreds more onto the shores of New Jersey's Liberty State Park.

By early afternoon, the downtown area was cordoned off; guarded by 2000 National Guardsmen and State Police. They had been called upon by New York Governor George Pataki.

It was a city under siege.

******

Over 50,000 people worked at the World Trade Center, and 10,000 in each tower alone. Thousands of people were severely injured and over six thousand died; Six thousand innocent men and women, husbands and wives, mothers and fathers, daughters and sons, all buried beneath the tower of rubble.

Marsh & McLennan, an insurance brokerage firm, reported that 1200 of its 1700 employees were unaccounted for. Cantor Fitzgerald, a bond firm, said 730 people of its 1000-person staff were missing.

*****

Even after the second tower collapsed, many remained alive beneath the rubble. The operators at 911 were receiving dozens of calls from people apparently buried and trapped in the debris.

Brian Jones, a 911 operator, reported that "one man said he was still trapped under the World Trade Center and said he was there along with two New York City sergeants."

"There are people that are still alive," New York Mayor Rudy Giuliani reported. "We'll be trying to recover as many people as possible and trying to clean up the horrible mess made by this."

After the south and then the north Towers of the World Trade Center had collapsed, firefighters began to organize yet another massive rescue effort. They set up a command post in 7 World Trade Center.

Rescue workers armed with shovels, spades, halogens and pickaxes again began to search for survivors and to recover bodies. Cranes 120 feet tall and bulldozers by the dozens were brought in to clear the debris. Governor Pataki mobilized the National Guard to help.

The Federal Health and Human Services Department activated a national medical emergency system in an attempt to mobilize 7000 doctors, nurses, paramedics and other medical personnel. They were to be rushed to the scene of chaos and carnage.

The National Association of Community Blood Centers sent 15,000 pints of blood to New York City. American citizens began lining up at blood banks all across the United States.

"There are a lot of burn victims," a Red Cross spokeswoman said. "They'll need platelets, plasma and red blood cells. That's why it's so important for people to give blood."

Over a thousand volunteers with medical or nursing experience formed rescue medical crews to provide immediate care for the injured.

Thousands of injured civilians, firefighters, police officers and rescue workers were taken to hospitals and medical facilities. Over 2000 injured people had been evaluated at a mobile hospital set up at Liberty State Park alone. Casualties were being treated at hospitals as far south as Toms River. Many had suffered crushing injuries, and severe and profound burns.

But still, even late that afternoon, there was a glimmer of hope that hundreds could be buried alive beneath the rubble.

Dogs trained to sniff out life were brought in.

These dogs are essential to any rescue and recovery operation, especially one so massive in scale. Dogs are social animals who with their acute sence of hearing and smell, are able to detect a wide range of sounds and smells, including the sound of breathing, movement, and the smell of life.

Dogs are incredibly useful in rescue operations and through their body language they can communicate the possibility that there may be life hidden beneath a mountain of debris. When they are positive, they will begin to dig.

They are hunters.

It comes natural to a dog to hunt for life. And as they love humans, it is especially rewarding to a dog if he finds a man or a woman, alive and buried beneath the rubble.

Like humans, who have for the last half million years up until the present, engaged in cooperate hunting, dogs and wolves are also essentially group hunters. Dogs are useful not only to hunters but to herdsman, farmers and modern humans as protector, loyal friend and for searching and aiding in the rescue of humans.

Hundreds of dogs were brought to New York on the afternoon and evening of September 11, 2001. And these dogs and their handlers immediately began sifting through the rubble, sniffing and searching for sparks of life. It is a dangerous job. Several of the dogs were injured. Some were crushed by shifting debris. Their paws were cut, their feet were injured and many were becoming depressed by the unending smell of death.

Dogs have feelings too.

Rescue dogs love humans. It gives them as much joy as their human counterpart to find and rescue a human being. And they eagerly go about their work, risking their own lives and sometimes losing their lives in the service of human beings.

That evening, one dog fell 100 feet. He had to be shot to death by his handler. Another fell 50 feet and suffered the same fate.

"Wuss" a 70-pound Beligan Malinois rescue dog, owned by Chris Christensten, was enveloped in a cloud of dust and could no longer breathe after entering a small jagged passage beneath the rubble of the World Trade Center.

Chris reeled him in, he was on a 15 foot leash.

"He had inhaled a lot of dust. He couldn't breath. His tongue was turning purple. I tried to give him oxygen... but Wuss went into shock..."

Yet, even when injured, even when totally exhausted, many of the dogs and their handlers push on. The handlers are usually more worried about their dogs than themselves, but on this night, both put themselves at risk, in order to save lives.

"I'm going till I can't go no more, till the dog can't go no more," said Joaquin Guerrero, a K-9 officer.

Likewise, Frank Coughlin, No. 5's captain, had no intention of giving up. "We'll have members at that scene until we bring all our guys home," Coughlin said.

When the dog sniffs out signs of life, they start digging, often tearing away at their paws. But on this night, there is little digging.

Rescue workers were warned they could expect to find very few survivors.

They knew they would find hundreds if not thousands of dead bodies. Police were forced to establish an 185,000 square-foot temporary morgue on a Hudson River pier.

"I lost count of all the dead people I saw," said firefighter Rudy Weindler, who spent nearly 12 hours trying to find survivors. "It is absolutely worse than you could ever imagine."

Hundreds more would die, trapped beneath the rubble, as they waited in vain to be rescued. But the heat of the fires made rescue impossible.

Even late that night, September 11, 2001, numerous fires were burning amid the disaster area. Temperatures in some areas were above 1500 degrees, due to the burning pools of jet fuel which were flaming up everywhere among the rubble.

The streets around where the World Trade Center once stood, were thick with broken vehicles and the remnants of buildings squashed, as if an asteroid had landed on them—some of them on fire.

The 1350-foot-tall World Trade Center Towers, one of the tallest buildings in the United States and the pride of New York, had been reduced to smoldering mountain of rubble; and into the evening, the fires still burned.

And not just the World Trade Center. Many of the surrounding buildings were also damaged and burning. And people lived and worked in those buildings. And many of them were injured and killed.

"There are so many other buildings that are partially de-stroyed and near collapse," said firefighter Weindler. "There are a lot of fires still burning."

It was a ring of unending fires. It was the fiery bottomless pits beyond the gates of hell.

The air reeked of jet fuel and burning rubber. Crushed and burned-out cars and buses clogged the streets and there were occasional explosions as cars blew up, one by one.

And then, just a few minutes after 5 p.m., yet another burning building, 7 World Trade Center, collapsed. It had become the temporary headquarters for the city's emergency command center.

It's collapse was sudden and completely unexpected. The building began to teeter, the windows started popping out and then it just collapsed, killing dozens of firemen including William Feehan, the First Deputy Fire Commissioner, and Peter Ganci, the Fire Department's Chief.

Again, rescuers tore at the rubble to free their friends and colleagues. But instead they found another mountain of death.

Heavy cranes lifted and moved aside concrete blocks and 40 foot steel beams that were impaled in the sidewalks.

It was a nightmare moonscape of death and destruction.

And still they searched, hoping to find survivors.

"There are people still alive in there," one firefighter said. "There's got to be."

But search as they might, they found only death and more death.

"There's part of a body over there," one fireman said point-ing at a jumble of twisted beams. "And over there. Body parts. Pieces. There are no signs of life. None. Everybody is dead. There is no way they could live through that. It's only going to be bod-ies coming out. Bodies and more bodies."

It would be nearly impossible for anyone to survive the fires, lying beneath the crush of thousands of pounds of concrete and steel.

Yet, some survived.

A Port Authority officer who had been on the 80th floor,

actually rode the building down as it collapsed, sliding a thousand feet. He survived beneath the rubble in an air pocket which let him breathe. He suffered only a broken leg.

A miracle perhaps.

Miracles do happen.

A police officer was found beneath the twisted steel girders and a thousand tons of concrete and tortured steel. He had ridden the collapse all the way down from the 86th floor. They found him at 1 a.m. and a call went out for a surgeon. They would have to amputate one leg to free him, and then, another miracle, they managed to extricate and save his left leg.

But even those who managed to survive beneath the rubble often die over the following days-of shock, severe burns, loss of blood, suffocation, organ damage and broken hearts.

That evening, refrigeration trucks began to arrive to handle the scores of bodies expected to be exhumed.

By the following day, a total of six people had been pulled from the rubble alive.

Over six thousand had died.

******

THE BUCKET BRIGADES

The search for bodies would continue for days.

As described by James Croak: "Spread out across the debris field are bucket brigades, serpentine chains of two hundred people each, firemen, cops, military lines meandering up and down to where the dig is taking place. The entire site is being excavated into five gallon pails, which are hand passed to dump trucks. Not a finger will be lost."

"Each dig has a cadaver dog, the dog shows us where to dig and then a small hole is made. In goes a TV camera with a listening device and everybody yells to be quiet. Generators go off and everyone stands still. After four days there are no more sounds."

"Now the digging and cutting begins."

"When they find a body they yell 'body coming' and an adjacent brigade climbs across the wreckage to form an opposing line. The body is then passed in a stretcher between the lines. If it is a fireman, his hat is placed atop him and the stretcher is carried, not passed."

"My first body was a fireman. His hat told me what had happened to him. Crushed, burned, shattered,. He looked to have been brought up from the sea, a civil war relic."

"My second body was a young girl, petite, in shape. 'I can't take this,' I thought, and considered running."

"Thankfully we didn't have another body for an hour or so. Periodically, the line would call 'we need paint,' meaning they found a body too deep to dig for at this time. So the area is sprayed red so we can find him later."

"Several times, we passed a body the size of a basket ball."

"If the wreckage shifts, a Klaxon blows twice telling everyone to run, which we do. A minute later we all run back, me still shaking."

"The next body was in a fetal position. She must have lived awhile, I thought, and died of exposure with a billion tons of mess on top of her, scared beyond understanding."

"In total, we found 27 bodies and carried out 9.

"You think there are no heroes in America? I saw a lanky blond that could have modeled Chanel, tie a rope around her ankle, grab a stethoscope and dive head first down a debris hole that would have shredded a raccoon. I saw firemen so deep into the rubble their flashlights were mistaken for fire. The firemen in general were fearless, shrugging their shoulders at the obvious danger of it all."

"But missing from the scene was any talk of how it got like this, why it came down, what should be done about it. Nothing, not a peep. I suspect that it was a kind of collective shame for not having protected us from this."

AFTERMATH:
THE HOME OF THE BRAVE

The twin attacks on the World Trade Center on September 11, 2001 left over 6000 people dead and unaccounted for.

The city had become a ghost town.

From the distance, one could still see the thick columns of smoke rising from the wreckage. Several stories of burnt steel, an empty shell of the steel structure's trademark design, stood tilted and in ruin.

The streets of Lower Manhattan, notorious for their traffic jams and crowds of people, were empty and eerily silent.

On the day of the attack, airports were closed. Trains and ferries stopped running. Bridges and tunnels were blocked. All ways into and out of the area were sealed off. Some walked for three hours, for ten miles, anything to get back to their homes.

New York City, accustomed to mobility and immediate transportation was paralyzed.

That was the first day.

On the day of September 11, New York became a different town.

"Everyone's devastated." said Detective Lisa Guerrero, a New York Police Department spokeswoman.

"It's the most horrific scene I've ever witnessed in my whole life," Mayor Rudolph Giuliani said.

In the first few days and weeks after the tragedy, the air still smelled like putrifying death, even from miles away.

This awful perfume greeted people as they awakened, making them remember and relive the devastation on what otherwise, would have been a beautiful morning.

Now it was a city in mourning.

And on the first morning, the depression of sadness spread.

Residents in Brooklyn found charred pieces of paper, discarded memos and spreadsheets that had blown across the river and found solace in their backyards.

So many lives, snuffed out and reduced to scraps of paper whispering in the wind... whispering of sadness and death.

Authorities were stringent against allowing anyone to return to the areas of devastation. People driven from their homes and apartments by the clouds of destruction, were told they could not return until the evidence had been collected.

Lower Manhattan, now the graveyard of thousands of murdered men and women, was considered a "crime scene." The authorities were not letting anybody in.

Monika Caha, a chef who resided in the downtown area for more than 15 years, told the New York Times, "Most people think of the area as a place for business and don't realize that there were thousands of people who've been living down here. For the last week we have basically been homeless and invisible."

In tears, residents pleaded with police to allow them to grab just a few things, to pick up photographs or just their child's favorite toy or security blanket. But under strict orders and the threat of national security, no exceptions could or would be allowed. The area was to be cleared of all civilians.

And orders, from the highest authorities, must be followed, even if homelessness for thousands would result in the end.

Amy Strassler, 35, a social studies teacher at the High School for Leadership and her husband Matthew Goldstein and their 22-month-old twin sons Trevor and William, were suddenly homeless. They began staying with friends and family and were uncertain of when they would be allowed to move into their home on Liberty street. Strassler, however, was not worried about her apartment and said, "You don't have anything to be angry or sad about when the people close to you are still alive." "There are so many people to be sorry about. Living out of a suitcase for six to eight weeks is nothing compared to what has happened," her husband, Matthew Goldstein told the Daily News.

After some time, the area was reopened to residents and they were given five minutes to gather up some possessions and belongings. Still they were only allowed access to their homes downtown, if they could provide proof that they belonged.

Welcome to the new America.

Police and state troopers checked identification of residents vigilantly for proof of address.

After days had gone by, and the danger had seemed to wane, some residents were permitted to move back into their homes. But many no longer wanted to live there. They only wanted to gather family photographs and other treasured keepsakes. One banker, who lived nearby the Trade Center, said, "I don't want to live here anymore. We've got a graveyard right across the street!"

A graveyard of six thousand souls.

New Yorkers have slowly begun picking up the pieces of their lives. The men and women wearing suits, ready for business are still on Wall Street. But things have changed. New York is a different city.

People were wearing face masks to work, shielding themselves from the particle-filled and putrid smelling air emanating from Ground Zero, two blocks away. National Guardsmen—armed soldiers with machine guns, garbed in camouflage green, guarded the Ground Zero site. One soldier, Sgt. Mitchel Visintin, who was manning a 60-mm machine gun atop a Hum-vee, told a New York paper, "It's just a presence, we're not going to use it on anyone. We're all armed and we're here to make everyone feels secure."

It wasn't working. The presence of so many police just made people more afraid; it was a constant reminder: everyone was in danger.

Police officers were noticeable on every corner directing traffic and pedestrians. Bomb scares abounded. Shortly after the World Trade Center's collapse, the Empire State Building was evacuated. Grand Central Station—a major hub of transportation, as well as other train stations, were being threatened. Entire neighborhoods and busy streets were cleared out.

According to Mayor Giuliani, New York, which normally gets about seven legitimate bomb threats a day, was getting about a hundred.

Over the following days, frozen mass transportation remained in disaray. The subway lines running below the World Trade Center, as well as the New Jersey Path Train, were not running downtown. Although the area has been reopened to pedestrians, it was still inaccessible to most vehicular traffic including mass transportation.

Everyone was affected one way or another. Whether he or she lost a loved one in the tragedy, or had to alter a commute to work or who knew someone who had been touched by loss.

Daily routines were drastically altered. Once effortless tasks like picking up prescriptions from the drug store, buying bread and milk —now in short supply— became missions. Downtown Manhattan was experiencing the effects of war.

"You get attached," one woman explained. "I walked through the World Trade Center two or three times a day, went to the Gap and bought my chocolate truffles there, went to the movies there," she said. "If I think about it, I could just cry."

"I won't let it get me down," Milton Fuller, Senior Vice President of Insurance at Morgan Stanley, told the Daily News. Fuller was working at the World Trade Center when the jets struck, and was also there for the first bombing in 1993. "What I learned from the first bombing in 93, was that if you get too mesmerized by the danger, then you'll change your life and it will probably be worse. You don't want to live life affected by fear. Then you'll be yielding to the terrorist mentality."

But some couldn't help but experience fear. Many continue to experience fear, even in areas far away from New York.

The hijackers had delivered a message. The message was fear: This war has just begun.

In Los Angeles, Dennison Samaroo, an actor and makeup artist, began stocking up on survival supplies. "I don't want to die because there's poison in my tap water —if I have my own water supply for a while, I can live. I can wait until the tap water clears or until I can travel elsewhere," he told the Los Angeles Times News Service: "This is not paranoia. It's about prepared-ness, not paranoia. It's about learning to cope with a new real-ity."

Renee Evans, 57, began stockpiling canned goods and wa-ter in her apartment in West Hollywood, California. She said, "I am terrified. It's all really scary. I'm putting up canned goods and water 'cause I don't know what's gonna happen next. They could mess with our food, our water supply. We'd be sitting ducks. I haven't been sleeping too much. I've been watching, praying and trying to figure out what we can do."

Many others across the country and in parts of New York like Long Island, were purchasing shot guns. Army and navy sur-plus stores found themselves selling out of survival kits, gas masks and containment suits.

There is fear and danger in the air. We have been wounded, taken unawares.

Americans are preparing for war, to survive the next attack.

New Yorkers, meanwhile, have the additional task of endur-ing a tragedy that has struck in their own home. A tragedy which they never imagined, actually happened to their city, "the great-est city in the world."

New Yorkers, known for their resilience, will perhaps never be known again for their rudeness or for being inconsiderate— but as a city wounded and in hurt.

The attitude in New York has changed. New Yorkers dropped their trademark brand of cynicism, rudeness, and nonchalance for patriotism. In the period following the attacks, they bran-dished the American flag proudly on their clothing, lined West Street to cheer emergency rescue workers in ambulances as they zoomed by. For the first time in their lives they thought twice

261

about cutting off other cars or honking their horns in city traffic.

People called old friends, ex-lovers and acquaintances to see if they were okay. New Yorkers took in displaced friends, sometimes even strangers, into their homes.

New York shops, which usually cater to tourists, found native New Yorkers buying American flags. The famous postcards of the World Trade Center and the impressive Manhattan skyline sold out from every souvenir shop.

Expressions of sorrow, patriotism and anger adorned every wall and window all over New York City. Flags flew at half staff. They could also be seen in nearly every store window, waving from cars and worn by joggers and travelers.

All across America, Americans, patriotic to the core, were behaving much the same.

Generosity was in excess. The Jacob Javits Convention Center became Volunteer Headquarters. Long lines snaked around the block and New Yorkers waited for more than two hours to fill out a form, offering any assistance, anything that was needed.

So many people wanted to help they had to be turned away. Supplies were overstocked. The blood supply could not contain any more donations.

Makeshift memorials arose spontaneously on street corners, store windows, on lamp posts of busy intersections. And in New York City's outer boroughs such as Brooklyn and Queens, the sentiment was no less patriotic. Signs and posters scrawled in marker cried out: "God Bless America" and "We Will Remember."

In front of a Staten Island Waterfront, from the shores of which can be viewed the disfigured New York skyline, there are hundreds of flowers, flags, letters and sympathy cards.

Union Square Park was transformed into the city's largest memorial, with candles blazing on the edges of every walkway through the park. Singers sang, gathering enthusiastic crowds, leading them in mournful and hopeful song.

Those who have lost loved ones take solace in these memorials as they wait and hope to hear news of a rescue or a recovery. Wives, husbands, sons, daughters, mothers, fathers, and friends made rounds at the hospital, holding up photos and flyers with pictures of their loved ones. Some are still unwilling to give up hope.

Firehouses have become the destination of pilgrimages, as people mournfully lay flowers and candles and write messages in journals, thanking these men who so bravely gave their lives.

At the somber promotion ceremony held to replace the Fire Department's top officers, who were killed in the World Trade Center's collapse, Rudolph Giuliani said, "Courage... And there is no better example, none, no better example of courage than the Fire Department of the City of New York...Courage... It's the most profound form of human love that we see displayed over and over again in our city."

Courage! In the aftermath of the brutal attacks on America, what we witnessed was courage: the courage of so many women and men who risked and sacrificed their lives to save the lives of their fellow Americans.

We are humbled. We are awed. We are inspired. We are honored that such men and women, the firemen, policemen, medical personnel, rescue workers, all these brave souls... that such men and women have lived among us, for by their selfless courage they have made us proud to be Americans.

THE HOME OF THE BRAVE

Two hundred years ago, on September 12, 1814, people from a foreign shore tried to take away America's freedom. Our nation was besieged by land, by sea, by air.

Missiles and rockets struck cities, destroying buildings, setting fires, and with much loss of life. Yet still the Americans fought with courage and tenacity.

On September 12, 1814, the young nation's third largest city, Baltimore, was besieged, and then when the attackers were forced to withdraw, they attacked again, by air and by sea.

Foreign ships bombarded Fort McHenry, which guarded Baltimore's shores. It was hell on earth, for 25 hours straight, but Major George Armistead, the fort's commander, refused to haul down the American flag. America would not surrender.

An American civilian held prisoner on an attacking ship, Francis Scott Key, watched anxiously through the night to see if in the morning the American flag was still flying high.

That morning he wrote:

O say can you see, by the dawn's early light,
What so proudly we hail'd at the twilight's last gleaming,
Whose broad stripes and bright stars through the perilous fight
O'er the ramparts we watch'd were so gallantly streaming?
And the rocket's red glare, the bombs bursting in air,
Gave proof through the night that our flag was still there.
O say does that star-spangled banner yet wave
O'er the land of the free and the home of the brave?

On the shore dimly seen through the mists of the deep
Where the foe's haughty host in dread silence reposes,
What is that which the breeze, o'er the towering steep,
As it fitfully blows, half conceals, half discloses?
Now it catches the gleam of the morning's first beam,
In full glory reflected now shines in the stream,
'Tis the star-spangled banner - O long may it wave
O'er the land of the free and the home of the brave!

And where is that band who so vauntingly swore,
That the havoc of war and the battle's confusion
A home and a Country should leave us no more?
Their blood has wash'd out their foul footstep's pollution.
No refuge could save the hireling and slave
From the terror of flight or the gloom of the grave,
And the star-spangled banner in triumph doth wave
O'er the land of the free and the home of the brave.

O thus be it ever when freemen shall stand
Between their lov'd home and the war's desolation!
Blest with vict'ry and peace may the heav'n rescued land
Praise the power that hath made and preserv'd us a nation!
Then conquer we must, when our cause it is just,
And this be our motto - "In God is our trust."

And the star-spangled banner
in triumph shall wave
Over the land of the free
and the home
of the
brave!

******

COMING SOON

TERRORISM:

THE FUTURE WARS AGAINST AMERICA

Edited by
Sara Jess, Gabriel Beck, R. Joseph

America is under attack. Is our drinking water safe? Will terrorists unleash nightmarish biological weapons in the cities of America? Are "friendly" nations planning nuclear war again the United States? Will American citizens be attacked by genetically engineered diseases and viruses? Will our cities be destroyed by "suitcase nukes"— nuclear bombs so small they can be smuggled inside the luggage of a terrorist?

America is under attack.

Coming soon from University Press, California.

Astrobiology, The Origin of Life and the Death of Darwinism

ISBN# 0-9700733-0-5
University Press, California

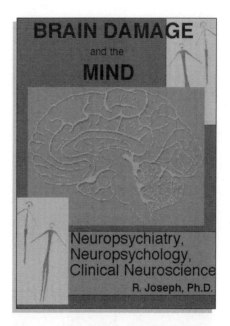

Brain Damage and the Mind
ISBN# 0-9700733-5-6
University Press, California

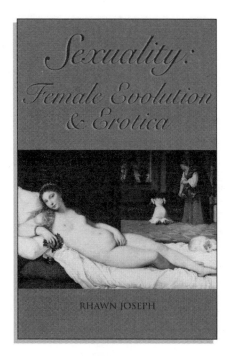

Sexuality:
Female Evolution and Erotica
ISBN# 0-9700733-6-4
University Press, California

6525

The Transmitter to God
The Limbic System, The Soul and Spirituality
ISBN# 0-9700733-3-13
University Press, California

Hitler's Diaries
The Mind & God of Adolf Hitler
ISBN# 0-9700733-9-9
University Press, California